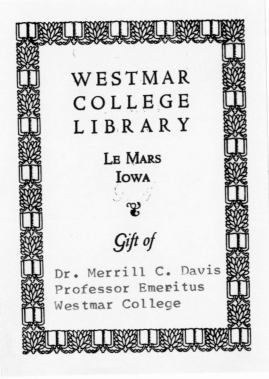

The History of Religions

ESSAYS IN METHODOLOGY

THE HISTORY OF
RELIGIONS

Essays in Methodology

EDITED BY

Mircea Eliade
and
Joseph M. Kitagawa

WITH A PREFACE BY

Jerald C. Brauer

THE UNIVERSITY OF CHICAGO PRESS

CHICAGO & LONDON

International Standard Book Number: 0-226-20394-8

Library of Congress Catalog Card Number: 59-11621

The University of Chicago Press, Chicago 60637
The University of Chicago Press, Ltd., London

© *1959 by The University of Chicago. All rights reserved. Published 1959*
Fifth Impression 1970
Printed in the United States of America

In Memory of

JOACHIM WACH

1898–1955

Preface

The study of the history of religions appears to be at a critical point in its development. This is true of the discipline both in the East and in the West. For decades it seemed ready to come into its own as a major area of study in the universities and colleges. At a few European institutions it achieved such a status, but in the universities of English-speaking countries and most European schools, it remained an honored but peripheral discipline. At best, history of religions found its place in a rather uncomfortable position between the social sciences and the humanities.

Today the history of religions will either develop into a major specialty, playing a key role within and between the social sciences, humanities, and theology, or it will lapse into respectably tolerated standing within one or several of these disciplines. It is to be hoped that the former alternative will prevail, and already numerous signs indicate that this will be the case.

It is a most auspicious period for the history of religions to become one of the pre-eminent disciplines in university life. It has more to offer both Eastern and Western man than ever before. The world condition is such that modern man, of the East and of the West, is struggling to comprehend this revolutionary age, with its sweeping changes and newly emerging patterns of life. One way in which man seeks to understand the present is to see it in relation to the past out of which it comes.

The world's religions are everywhere resurgent. For the first time in modern history, Christianity, the predominant faith of the West, is faced by reinvigorated Eastern religions. This development can be explained only partially by the rising Eastern nationalism. The fact is that Western man cannot understand or appreciate the Asian peoples unless he has some knowledge and understanding of their religions. This in itself puts history of religions on a new footing in the modern university. It is no longer merely an interesting, esoteric, but respected pursuit.

The history of religions is now necessary to apprehend our world situation and thus ourselves.

Another factor that has brought about this change in attitude toward the discipline is the new perspective that has been at work for the past quarter-century and is now beginning to dominate the mind and spirit of much of Western mankind. This new perspective grows out of developments in science, anthropology, and theology, but it is certain to expand in counteraction to a false equalitarianism. It upholds the uniqueness and givenness of vast expanses of human experience. Unlike the approach which seeks to reduce all experience and reality to a few basic ingredients or principles, this new perspective strives to grasp a given reality in its own terms, in its own uniqueness, and in its own context. Basic similarities are not stressed at the expense of peculiarities or differences.

Not only has the history of religions gone through this basic shift in viewpoint, as demonstrated by Professors Kitagawa and Smith, but it has helped to establish and deepen the new perspective. Religions are to be studied and understood for their own sake and not simply to provide self-knowledge, social knowledge, or ammunition to uphold a given religion. To be sure, all these things will be done, and therefore ought to be done with skill, imagination, and method, but at its best the history of religions goes beyond any one of these functions. It seeks to penetrate one of the few cardinal facts of life—the phenomenon of man as a religious being. To properly investigate and explore this fundamental, one must begin with an attitude of respect and openness toward the religious reality itself as it is encountered in specific historical forms.

It is interesting to note that at this moment in history, when people everywhere are called upon to understand the heritage of others, a perspective dominates in the history of religions that demands investigation from a point of view that takes seriously the uniqueness and particularity of each historical religion. The discipline does not give up the search for universals or types, but it has moved far beyond the possibility of locating these in a few clear moral, ethical, or national common denominators. It can be argued that the enterprise now seeks the basically religious by moving through individual historical religious experiences rather than by ignoring or moving around the peculiar or particular experiences. Thus the discipline has much to contribute to modern self-understanding and will make its impact felt increasingly in university education.

In spite of the favorable contemporary circumstances, it will not be easy for the history of religions to establish itself as one of the leading scholarly activities in the modern university. In fact, the great danger is that it will be completely absorbed by certain other fields. The history of religions deals with materials handled also by philosophy of religion, psychology, sociology, anthropology, history and theology. Its problem is to demonstrate that it is not merely ancillary to these other studies but is a discipline in its own right, drawing upon, yet making unique additions to, these areas of knowledge.

This is the question with which Professors Eliade, Daniélou, Pettazzoni, and Massignon wrestle. It is the question of the methodology appropriate to the discipline. Unless a satisfactory answer can be found concerning the content and method adapted to the history of religions, it will not be able to fulfil its potential role. The late Professor Joachim Wach was probably correct in stating that there is no single procedure forever suitable to the study of the history of religions but that the method will have to be adequate to the total epoch and prevailing conditions of the time to which the study is directed. That is the point at which this discipline has now arrived. The essays of Daniélou and Eliade make this quite clear.

On the other hand, there appears to be a good deal of effort in this undertaking to develop a satisfactory method and thereby to make its contributions. That is the purpose of this volume. Faced by an almost incomprehensible amount of material always contained in the most complex linguistic, political, and social contexts, the history of religions has moved ahead in the attempt to mark out its own responsibilities and contributions. It is as aware as any other discipline of the tension between objectivity and subjectivity, and it too is fighting the battle to achieve balance between unavoidable specialization and the necessity for generalization.

Scholarship in the United States sustains a notable burden in these circumstances, not only because of its unmatched financial resources, but also because of its unique position as the middle ground between European culture and the culture of the Asian nations. In this central situation American scholarship should be eager and willing to play a new role. Because of the vast amount of research in the social sciences, American universities are especially well equipped to become great centers for the study of the history of religions. They must of necessity retain a close connection with European universities while at the same time they develop and expand relations with the East and Africa.

One further practical consideration places a special obligation on American institutions. The history of religions faces increasing demands throughout American colleges and universities, but the reasons for this are not all good. Nevertheless, this presents a golden opportunity for the history of religions to seize the initiative and to turn it in the right direction. It could become as universal and as necessary a study for the college or university student as is mathematics or history. We live in the kind of world that compels us in the direction of such a movement.

It is planned to produce additional volumes in a series on the history of religions in order that specialists and other scholars may be kept abreast of developments in this investigation. An attempt will be made to focus on the major problems and areas of interest in the particular field, but an endeavor will also be made to deal with the interrelations of the history of religions to other disciplines.

It is fitting that the editorial work for this volume was done and two of the essays written by Professor Eliade and by Professor Kitagawa, a former student of the late Joachim Wach. Professor Wach was determined to build a strong discipline of the history of religions in the midst of a great American university. As his writings demonstrate, he was concerned that the question of method take temporary precedence over other aspects of study. He felt this was necessary if it was to survive as a distinct discipline and to play the creative role to which the history of religions was called by this era.

Mircea Eliade, Wach's successor as chairman of the field of the history of religions in the theological faculty of the University of Chicago, continues in his own unique way the concern that the discipline develop and exhibit a method adequate to its own content, problems, and materials. It was to be expected that the first in a series of volumes on the history of religions edited by these scholars would deal with the central problem of methodology.

JERALD C. BRAUER

Contents

JOSEPH M. KITAGAWA

The History of
Religions in America

I

On the sixtieth birthday of Gerardus van der Leeuw, Joachim
Wach dedicated to him an essay "On Teaching History of Religions."[1] In this essay, Wach noted that there was no one way
or method which could be handed down from one generation of
scholars and teachers to the next, because the approach will have
to be adapted to the specific needs of each generation and different conditions prevailing in different countries. Considering the
fact that increasing numbers of educational institutions in
America are offering courses in the history of religions and related subjects, it may be worthwhile for us to reflect on the nature and the scope of the discipline, and discuss some of the
relevant problems relating to the research and teaching in the
field of the history of religions or *Religionswissenschaft* in
America.

It is significant to note that the discipline of the history of
religions, in the sense the term is used in the present article, did
not develop in America until a relatively recent date. This may
be due, in part at least, to the religious background of America.
During the Colonial period, America witnessed the introduction

[1] Joachim Wach, "On Teaching History of Religions," *Pro regno pro
sanctuario*, ed. Willem J. Kooiman (Nijkerk: G. F. Callenbach, 1950), pp.
525–32.

1

of various types of European church groups. In the course of time American cultural experience, coupled with the influence of pietism, revivalism, and rationalism, resulted in the principle of religious liberty, which enabled Americans of diverse confessional backgrounds to live together in relative peace. In this situation the religious problems which were relevant to Americans centered around the relations among different ecclesiastical groups—between Protestantism and Catholicism, and between Christianity and Judaism. Tales were told of other religions in far-off lands, but religions other than Judeo-Christian traditions presented no real alternative and thus did not concern the citizens of the new republic. To be sure, there was one Bostonian, Hannah Adams (d. 1832), who wrote on such topics as "A Brief Account of Paganism, Mohometanism, Judaism, and Deism," and "A View of the Religions of the Different Nations of the World," but she was a rare exception.

In the latter half of the nineteenth century, however, interest in religions of the world became rather widespread in America. Philosophers, theologians, philologists, historians, and ethnologists began to be fascinated by the so-called comparative approach. In the year 1867, James Freeman Clarke was called to the chair of natural religion and Christian doctrine in the Harvard Divinity School. His *Ten Religions: An Essay in Comparative Theology* dealt with the historical origin and development of individual religions as well as the historical survey of certain key ideas and doctrines, such as doctrines of God, man, and salvation. Another pioneer in this field was a Unitarian minister, Samuel Johnson, whose book *Oriental Religions and Their Relations to Universal Religion* was indicative of the cultural climate of his day. In 1873 Boston University invited William Fairfield Warren, author of *The Quest of the Perfect Religion*, to become its first professor of comparative theology and of the history and philosophy of religion. Crawford Howell Toy's *Judaism and Christianity* and Frank Field Ellinwood's *Oriental Religions and Christianity* were also read in the same period. Parenthetically, Ellinwood, who was professor of comparative religion at New York University, was instrumental in organizing the American Society of Comparative Religion in 1890. Other books which appeared in the latter part of the nineteenth century include James Clement Moffat's *A Comparative History of*

Religions (1871), Samuel Henry Kellog's *The Light of Asia and the Light of the World* (1885), David James Burrell's *The Religions of the World* (1888), Edward Washburn Hopkins' *Religions of India* (1895) and *The Great Epics of India* (1901), William Dwight Whitney's *Max Müller and the Science of Language* (1892), George Stephen Goodspeed's *A History of the Babylonians and Assyrians* (1902), and William James's *The Varieties of Religious Experience* (1902).[2]

In the year 1881, Princeton Theological Seminary established a chair in the relations of philosophy and science to the Christian religion, and in 1891 Cornell University appointed a professor of the history and philosophy of religion and Christian ethics, and Harvard University called George Foot Moore to the chair of the history of religions. In 1892 the University of Chicago established the Department of Comparative.Religion and called George Stephen Goodspeed to teach comparative religion and ancient history. In the same year Brown University inaugurated a chair in natural theology. Also in 1892 a committee representing Columbia, Cornell, Johns Hopkins, Pennsylvania, Yale, and other leading institutions established "The American Lectures on the History of Religions" for the purpose of encouraging scholarly presentation on various aspects of the religions of the world. It is also to be noted that in 1895 the University of Chicago established the Haskell (annual) and Barrows (triennial) lectureships, and in 1897 the American Oriental Society formed a section for the historical study of religions. In 1899 Union Theological Seminary, New York, joined other institutions in establishing a chair on the philosophy and history of religions.

By far the most dramatic event to stimulate American interest in the religions of the world was the World Parliament of Religions, held in Chicago in 1893 in connection with the Columbian Exposition. Its motto was:

To unite all Religion against all irreligion; to make the Golden Rule the basis of this union; to present to the world . . . the substantial unity of many religions in the good deeds of the Religious Life; to provide for a World's Parliament of Religions, in which their common aims and common grounds of unity may be set forth, and the marvelous Religious progress of the Nineteenth century be reviewed. . . .[3]

[2] Louis Henry Jordan, *Comparative Religion, Its Genesis and Growth* (Edinburgh: T. & T. Clark, 1905), pp. 197 ff.

[3] The World's Religious Congress, *General Programme* (preliminary ed.; 893), p. 19.

The parliament had a far-reaching effect on the American scene. Something of the nature of the parliament is indicated by the fact that the general committee, under the chairmanship of John Henry Barrows (Presbyterian), included William E. McLaren (Episcopal), David Swing (Independent), Jenkin Lloyd Jones (Unitarian), P. A. Feehan (Catholic), F. A. Noble (Congregational), William M. Lawrence (Baptist), F. M. Bristol (Methodist), E. G. Hirsch (Jew), A. J. Canfield (Universalist), M. C. Ranseen (Swedish Lutheran), J. Berger (German Methodist), J. W. Plummer (Quaker), J. Z. Torgersen (Norwegian Lutheran), L. P. Mercer (New Jerusalem, Swedenborgian), and C. E. Cheney (Reformed Episcopal). In addition to the representatives of the Christian and Jewish bodies, representatives of Islam, Hinduism, Buddhism, and other religious faiths were invited to come and "present their views of the great subjects of religious faith and life." Each group was asked to make the best and most comprehensive statement of the faith it holds and the service it claims to have rendered to mankind. "All controversy is prohibited. No attack will be made on any person or organization. Each participating body will affirm its own faith and achievements, but will not pass judgment on any other religious body or system of faith or worship."[4] Significantly, at the last union meeting of the parliament, E. G. Hirsch spoke on "Universal Elements in Religion," William R. Alger on "The Only Possible Method for the Religious Unification of the Human Race," J. G. Schurman on "Characteristics of the Ultimate Religion," George Dana Boardman on "Christ the Unifier of Mankind," and Merwin-Marie Snell on "The Future of Religion."

Among the participants were many notable scholars, including historians of religions, but they attended the parliament as representatives of their faiths or denominations and not of the discipline of the history of religions. Nevertheless, in the minds of many Americans, comparative religion and the cause of the World Parliament of Religions became inseparably related. What interested many ardent supporters of the parliament was the religious and philosophical inquiry into the possibility of the unity of all religions, and not the scholarly, religio-scientific study of religions. Nevertheless, the history of religions and

4 *Ibid.*, p. 20.

4

comparative religion, however they might be interpreted, became favorite subjects in various educational institutions in America. Even the established churches took keen interest in these subjects. For example, the conference of the Foreign Mission Boards of the Christian Churches of the United States and Canada in 1904 recommended that theological schools of all denominations provide for missionary candidates courses of instruction in comparative religion and the history of religions.[5]

Undoubtedly, the widespread acceptance of the study of comparative religion or the history of religions in American universities and seminaries from the turn of the century was greatly aided by religious liberalism. Professor George F. Thomas suggests two reasons for the popularity of these subjects. First, the history of religions was considered a science and was thus regarded neutral in the conflict between Christianity and other religions. Second, religious liberalism stressed the continuity of Christianity with other religions and preferred the philosophical to the theological approach to the subject of religion. Many liberals were convinced that the philosophy of religion could pronounce conclusions about religious questions without Christian presuppositions.[6] In short, Christian liberalism was "an expression of the Christian faith in the one human community under the reign of God."[7] Many liberals were naïvely optimistic about social progress as well as the "stuff of human brotherhood" crossing religious lines.

This tendency favorable to the history of religions and comparative religion has been reversed since the middle of the 1930's, partly under the influence of the theological renaissance and partly because of the change which has taken place in cultural and educational domains. Philosophers, theologians, and social scientists who formerly were fascinated by the comparative approach to the study of world religions have begun to question the validity of such an approach. Not a few of them go even so far as to deny the integrity of *Religionswissenschaft* or the history of religions as an academic discipline. At the risk of over-

[5] Jordan, *op. cit.*, p. 375.

[6] George F. Thomas, "The History of Religion in the Universities," *Journal of Bible and Religion*, Vol. XVII (1949).

[7] Daniel Day Williams, *What Present-Day Theologians Are Thinking* (New York: Harper & Bros., 1952), p. 53.

5

simplification, let us cite four major criticisms of the history of religions.

First, some philosophers of religion hold that historians of religions are essentially philosophers of religion, or they ought to be if they are not already. To them, the religio-scientific inquiry of the history of religions is an important tool to develop an adequate philosophy of religion, which transcends the regional and subjective elements involved in all religious systems. Or, to put it differently, they may say that all religions are manifestations of, or a search for, one underlying primordial "religion" and the task of the history of religions is, in co-operation with the philosophy of religion, to study the relation between religion and religions and to enlighten a confused humanity so that it will eventually move toward the absolute truth.

Second, there are those who hold that the so-called objective approach of the history of religions is not objective enough, because of the very nature of the subject matter. Thus they urge historians of religions to concentrate more on the historical, phenomenological, and institutional aspects of religions, depending heavily on the co-operation and assistance of anthropologists, sociologists, philologists, and universal as well as regional historians.

There is a third group who hold that the history of religions does not take seriously enough the subjective elements involved in the study of various religions. They sometimes compare historians of religions, uncharitably to be sure, to "flies crawling on the surface of a goldfish bowl, making accurate and complete observations on the fish inside . . . and indeed contributing much to our knowledge of the subject; but never asking themselves, and never finding out, how it feels to be a goldfish."[8] What is important, according to this line of thinking, is to let the adherents of each religion speak for themselves about the nature of their own religious experiences, their views of the world and of life, and their own forms of beliefs and worship.

Finally, there are still others who rule out the possibility of religio-scientific approach to the study of religions on the grounds that each investigator is incurably conditioned by his own religious and cultural background. On this basis they advocate

[8] Wilfred Cantwell Smith, "The Comparative Study of Religion," *Inaugural Lectures* (Montreal: McGill University, 1950), p. 42.

the necessity of what might be termed as a theological history of religions, be it Islamic, Christian, or Hindu, as the only legitimate discipline. Closely related to this perspective is that of missiology or *Missionswissenschaft*, which utilizes the data and findings of *Religionswissenschaft* for apologetic purposes from the standpoint of Islamic, Christian, Buddhist, or Hindu faith.

All these criticisms have been raised by men and women in all walks of life. However, what concerns us particularly is the fact that the basic unclarity of the discipline of the history of religions has created confusion regarding the place of the history of religions in the academic curriculum in this country. Generally speaking, there are three kinds of educational institutions which are concerned with the teaching of the history of religions. In the undergraduate colleges and universities the question of the history of religions is discussed in connection with the problem of the teaching of religion. In the graduate institutions questions are raised as to the legitimacy of the history of religions as an academic discipline, and also the relations of the research method to other disciplines. In the theological schools and seminaries, the questions of the history of religions are involved in the relations of Christianity to other religions.

II

There are different kinds of undergraduate colleges in America, some private, some church-sponsored or church-related, and others are municipal or state institutions. Many of the state colleges and universities do not offer instruction in religion, while some of them provide courses dealing with the Bible, general surveys of religions of the world, and philosophical and ethical concepts of the Judeo-Christian traditions. The distinction between the private and church-related colleges is not always clear. A number of private colleges and universities were originally founded by church groups at the time when American religious life was strongly influenced by emotional revivalism. As a result, it was said in the last century that educated people had to choose between being intellectual and being pious, but found it difficult to be both simultaneously. In this historical context, one can appreciate the struggle of the educational institutions for the right of freedom of inquiry. Happily, today in most of the private colleges and universities teaching and research are free from ecclesiastical interference. At any rate, in some of the colleges there still remains an antireligious tradition, which began as a reaction against the earlier religious background of their institutions. It must also be remembered that until recently it was fashionable for intellectuals, both in the private and state institutions, to explain away religion.

Since World War II this situation has changed somewhat. The present religious scene in America is even described as an "Indian Summer of Religious Revival." In this situation, many educators, students, and parents ask: "What is the place of religion in the college curriculum?" Some people, while recognizing religion as a legitimate subject matter, maintain that religion is basically "caught" but not "taught," thus arguing against inclusion of courses in religion in the curriculum. Others, who admit the importance of religion in the curriculum, nevertheless have an instinctive fear that such a step might become the opening wedge of a wholesale invasion of religious groups into the academic institution. In this setting many questions are inevitably asked, such as whether or not the history of religions teaches religion, whether religions of the world can be or should be taught without value judgment, and finally whether the history of religions is to provide intellectual understanding about religions or contribute to the religious growth of students.

These questions are especially relevant to a program of general education. In many colleges, the first two years are devoted to general education and are followed by two years of a specialized program; in some others, both types of educational program are given side by side; in still others, the general education program is built in a pyramid fashion—for instance, three general education courses are taken in the first year, two in the second, and one each in the third and the fourth years. In the specialized program, it is taken for granted that there are a number of courses dealing with the subject matter of religion in one way or another, such as courses in sociology, anthropology, history, philosophy, literature, and the fine arts. But the place of the study of religion as such in the general education program is a subject of heated discussion and controversy.

The famous report of the Harvard Committee, published in 1945 under the title, *General Education in a Free Society*,[9] did

[9] Harvard Committee, *General Education in a Free Society* (Cambridge, Mass.: Harvard University Press, 1945).

8

not propose courses on religion as such. Instead, certain aspects of religion were included in the humanities and the social sciences. For example, in recommending a course on the study of the "heritage of philosophy in our civilization," the report said:

Western culture may be compared to a lake fed by the stream of Hellenism, Christianity, science, and these contributions might offer an extremely valuable way of considering the conceptions of a life of reason, the principle of an ordered and intelligible world, the ideas of faith, of a personal God, of the absolute value of the human individual, the method of observation and experiment, and the conception of empirical laws, as well as the doctrines of equality and of the brotherhood of man.[10]

The Harvard Committee also proposed a course within the social sciences on "Western Thought and Institutions," which was designed to examine the institutional and theoretical aspects of the Western heritage. In the words of the Committee:

The attempt is not to survey all history and all political and social thought but to open up some of the great traditions, to indicate the character of some attempted solutions of the past, to study a few of those topics and of the great statements of analysis or of ideals with some intensity.[11]

Columbia University's introductory courses on "Contemporary Civilization" are similar to the Harvard Committee's proposed course on "Western Thought and Institutions." Along this line, most colleges and universities in America offer courses in which the place of religion in Western history and culture is treated. It is a sound educational principle to discuss the writings of, say, Thomas Aquinas or Luther in the economic, social, and political context of their times, for in a real sense they were "great expressions of ideas which emanated from certain historical backgrounds."[12]

It is significant that today there is a definite trend toward offering courses in religion within the context of general education. A recent catalogue of Harvard University shows that all students are required to elect three elementary courses in general education, one to be chosen from each of three areas (humanities, social sciences, and natural sciences). The elementary courses in humanities include such titles as "Ideas of Good and Evil in Western Literature," and "Ideas of Man and the World

[10] *Ibid.*, p. 211.
[11] *Ibid.*, p. 216.   [12] *Ibid.*

9

in Western Thought." The second group of courses in humanities include such courses as "Classics of the Christian Tradition," "Classics of the Far East," "Introduction to the New
Testament," "New Testament Thought and the Mind of Today," "Religion and Culture," and "Roots of Western Culture."
The social sciences also offer an interesting variety of subjects,
such as "Natural Man and Ideal Man in Western Thought" and
"Freedom and Authority in the Modern World" in the elementary courses, and "History of Far Eastern Civilization," "Introduction to the Civilization of India," and "Introduction to
the Civilization of the Middle East" in the secondary group.[13]

This is not an isolated development at Harvard. Many colleges and universities offer at least one course in religion. "Typi-
cally," says Professor Harry M. Buck, Jr., "it is a three-hour
course in 'comparative religions' in which Christianity, Judaism
and all the religions of Asia are surveyed in a single semester by
lectures, textbook assignments and collateral readings." Buck
points out that "developments in the methodology [of the history of religions] have quite outstripped the practices in most
undergraduate institutions," and "the demands placed upon
instruction in this area in our own day compel a radical reap-
praisal of aims and methods."[14]

Who teaches such courses, and how are they administered?
Here, again, wide variety may be observed. Where there are
scholarly talents in specific religious and cultural areas, their
participation is solicited to form a team. More often than not,
however, what is nominally known as teamwork in teaching a
number of religions in a single course degenerates into a "cafe-
teria" system. On the other hand, a single teacher cannot be
expected to keep up with all the important researches in reference to many religions and cultures. To make the matter more
complex, in some institutions courses on world religions are
offered in the department of philosophy, in others in the departments of history or religion. In some cases, teachers with personal
interests, say a historian, linguist, anthropologist, philosopher,
biblical scholar, or a returned missionary, persuade the college
administrators to let them develop courses on world religions

[13] *Official Register of Harvard University*, LII, No. 20 (August, 1955), 19.

[14] Harry M. Buck, Jr., "Teaching the History of Religions," *Journal of
Bible and Religion*, XXV (October, 1957), 279.

under the titles of the history of religions or comparative religion. Although the accurate statistics are not yet available, it has been estimated by some that two to three hundred teachers, full-time or part-time, are engaged in teaching the history of religions in America, and nearly a hundred more may be added if we include Canada. All these teachers are wrestling with the question how best to teach the history of religions in the undergraduate setting.

We agree with Wach that there is not one way or one method of teaching, because the approach will have to be adapted to specific needs and different conditions. However, Wach's seven suggestions seem to be sound as general principles. He states that instruction in the history of religions must be (1) integral, (2) competent, (3) related to an existential concern, (4) selective, (5) balanced, (6) imaginative, and (7) adapted to various levels of instruction.[15] Buck also makes helpful suggestions, emphasizing the importance of (1) selectivity, (2) thoroughness in context, (3) comprehensiveness, and (4) a balanced perspective.[16] Far more urgent, however, is the clarification of the nature, scope, and method of the discipline of the history of religions itself. This is the problem which is debated heatedly in the context of the graduate program as much as in the undergraduate setting.

In a real sense, the chaotic picture of the undergraduate teaching of the history of religions can be traced to the lack of adequate graduate training centers for *Religionswissenschaft* in North America. Thus, when teachers of world religions are needed at many undergraduate colleges, they usually appoint either philosophers of religion, historians, biblical scholars, or theologians who happen to have personal interests and perhaps had taken two or three courses in the history of religions or comparative religion. If and when a person is trained solely in the general history of religions, he will have difficulty in fitting into the undergraduate teaching program. In retrospect, one is struck by the fact that the vogue of comparative religion, which started in the latter part of the last century and lasted until the 1920's, did not penetrate graduate institutions to the point of establishing strong centers of research and training in the field. Even where the so-called graduate departments of comparative reli-

[15] *Op. cit.*, pp. 528–30.   [16] *Op. cit.*, pp. 280–85.

11

gion were instituted, they usually centered around one or two scholars, who offered courses with the assistance of scholars in related fields.

In today's academic world, especially in the graduate institutions, scholarship implies specialized knowledge and competence. Unfortunately, from the standpoint of academic specialization the current teaching and research in the field of the history of religions appear to be ambiguous. The history of religions inherited the encyclopedic interest of the age of the Enlightenment. Its pioneers were interested and trained in several disciplines, such as philology, history, folklore, philosophy, and psychology. These "auxiliary" disciplines were regarded as necessary tools of research, to be called into service contemporaneously and employed by the same investigator. Today few, if any, can claim competence in all phases of the encyclopedic *Allgemeine Religionswissenschaft.* By necessity a historian of religions must concentrate on one or two of the auxiliary disciplines and also on special fields, such as primitive religion, antiquity, Middle Ages, modern period, or any one of the major religious systems. It is inevitable that those historians of religions majoring in specific areas are constantly rivaled by scholars outside the field of religion who are interested in the same areas. It has come to be taken for granted, for instance, that Islamicists, Indologists, Sinologists, and Japanologists are "specialists" of Islam, Hinduism, Chinese religions, and Shinto, respectively, and that anthropologists are "specialists" on primitive religion. Hence the "Memoirs of the American Anthropological Association" include such works as *Studies in Chinese Thought* (Memoir No. 75), *Studies in Islamic Cultural History* (Memoir No. 76), *Islam: Essays in the Nature and Growth of a Cultural Tradition* (Memoir No. 81), and *Village India* (Memoir No. 83). The scholars of these rival disciplines, equipped with adequate research personnel, facilities, and financial backing, are in a better position to pursue research in their endeavors than the historians of religions, and they often question the competence of the history of religions as an academic discipline.

It has also been observed that some disciplines are developing comprehensive outlooks, from their own perspectives, which often touch upon the problems that have been in the past dealt with in the systematic dimension of *Religionswissenschaft.* There

12

is no denying that philosophers such as Hocking, Radhakrishnan, and Northrop, missiologists like Kraemer, and historians like Toynbee have much to say on the subject of religions. It is but natural that many people ask whether or not historians of religions have a special contribution to make which these scholars cannot make.

Thus it is that in both the undergraduate colleges and the graduate institutions questions have been raised concerning the nature of the discipline of the history of religions. Similar questions are also viewed with the perspective of theological schools and seminaries. One of the main features of American theological institutions is that the overwhelming majority of them are denominationally oriented and autonomous institutions, loosely related or unrelated to graduate universities. Although theological study itself is supposed to be graduate work, for the most part it tends to emphasize professional preparation, concentrating on ministerial training. The majority of seminaries, with the exception of interdenominational graduate theological schools, have little access to universities, and thus are more sensitive to the movements within the churches than to the trends in the academic world.

Most seminaries in America consider either comparative religion or the history of religions as a tool for the Christian world mission. In this connection, it must be remembered that American denominations developed as missionary churches. While European churches generally depended on semiautonomous missionary societies for the missionary work abroad, most American churches accepted the missionary obligation as a task of the total church body. Starting with the formation of the Baptist missionary society in 1814, most major denominations established their own denominational missionary societies in the nineteenth century, and American churches played increasingly important roles in the domain of the Christian world mission. Some of the American missionaries were well trained in comparative religion, and they made significant contributions to scholarship. It is also to be noted, as stated earlier, that comparative religion was a favorite subject of American seminaries from the latter part of the nineteenth century to the 1920's.

Today, however, under the impact of a theological renaissance, American theological schools and seminaries are preoccupied with theology. Professor Nels Ferré analyzes the recent theological trends in America into two major kinds, those that stress objectivity and those that emphasize the subjective response. Under the former, he lists Fundamentalism, the High Church wing, and "Barthian" biblicism; under the latter, he discusses liberalism and existentialism.[17] Here we cannot go into the analyses of each of these trends or the adequacy of Ferré's interpretation of the recent trends in American theology, except to say that theologians of different persuasions, with the possible exception of the so-called liberals, while recognizing the usefulness of the history of religions, nevertheless agree with Professor Hendrik Kraemer in stating that only theology "is able to produce that attitude of freedom of the spirit and of impartial understanding, combined with a criticism and evaluation transcending all imprisonment in preconceived ideas and principles as ultimate standards of reference."[18] Such assertions imply that only those who view religions "from within" are competent to understand them. They do not exclude the validity of the history of religions; they insist, however, that the history of religions must for its own sake be aided by a theology.

Confronted by such serious questions and criticisms in the undergraduate colleges, graduate institutions, and theological seminaries, the history of religions is compelled to re-examine, from its own standpoint, its relation to other disciplines and in so doing to clarify the nature and scope of its own discipline.

III

The term the "history of religions" means different things to different people. To some it is a sort of Cooke's tour in world religions, in the sense that various aspects of religions are depicted and studied, using the comparative method. To others it is essentially a philosophical study of "religion" as it underlies all historical phenomena of various religions. To still others it is a historical discipline, analogous to church history, dealing with not only one religion but a number of religions. Is the history of religions a discipline auxiliary to philosophy of religion or to a social science? Or is it an autonomous discipline? And, if

[17] Nels F. S. Ferré, "Where Do We Go from Here in Theology?" *Religion in Life* (Winter, 1955/56).

[18] Hendrik Kraemer, *Religion and the Christian Faith* (Philadelphia: Westminster Press, 1956), p. 53.

so, does it belong to the theological curriculum or the humanities?

This apparent ambiguity of the nature of the discipline of the history of religions is reflected in the diversity of names by which it has come to be known, such as comparative religion, phenomenology of religion, science of religions, and history of religions. All these terms, with minor differences, refer to a general body of knowledge known originally as *Allgemeine Religionswissenschaft*. In the English-speaking world the imposing title of "general science of religions" has not been used widely, partly because it is too long and awkward, and partly because the English word "science" tends to be misleading. Thus, the world-wide organization of scholars in this field has recently adopted an official English title, "The International Association for the Study of the History of Religions." It is readily apparent that the term "history of religions" has come to be regarded as a synonym for the "general science of religions," and as such the nature of the discipline must be discussed in the total context of *Religionswissenschaft*.

It must be made abundantly clear that the history of religions is not proposed as the only valid method of studying religions. Actually, it is only one among many different approaches, such as philosophy of religion, psychology of religion, sociology of religion, and theology. Unlike philosophy of religion and theology, however, the history of religions does not "indorse" any particular system offered by the diverse religions of the world, nor does it advocate, as many ultra-liberals think it ought, any new universal synthetic religion. On the other hand, there are those who study other religions much as the commander of an invading army investigates enemy territory, and with much the same motivations. Such an approach is, of course, not acceptable to the history of religions, for this discipline does not prove the superiority of any particular religion over others.

There are three essential qualities underlying the discipline of the history of religions: First is a sympathetic understanding of religions other than one's own. Second is an attitude of self-criticism, or even skepticism, about one's own religious background. And third is the "scientific" temper.

Historically, the encounter of different peoples and religions has often resulted in serious conflicts and the subjugation of one

15

group by another, but in some cases it has also fostered sympathetic understanding and mutual respect among individuals of different backgrounds. Sometimes, knowledge of other religions, or a crisis in one's life, leads one to question one's own religious faith.

For example, in sixth century B.C. Greece the traditional faith in local gods began to be questioned for a number of reasons. Similar things happened in other parts of the world. In ancient times, however, questions about gods and religions were more often than not approached and solved "religiously" rather than "intellectually." Thus, the Hebrew god triumphantly challenged the skeptical man in the Book of Job:

> And the Lord said to Job:
> "Shall a faultfinder contend with the Almighty?
> He who argues with God, let him answer it."[19]

> Then Job answered the Lord:
> "I know that thou canst do all things,
> and that no purpose of thine can be thwarted,
> 'Who is this that hides counsel without knowledge?'
> Therefore I have uttered what I did not understand,
> things too wonderful for me, which I did not know."[20]

During the Middle Ages three monotheistic religions—Judaism, Christianity, and Islam—existed side by side in the Mediterranean area. The relationship among them was amazingly amiable in certain areas, and Christians, Jews, and Muslims had ample opportunities to "compare" their religions with others and ask serious questions. Indeed, some of them did ask fundamental questions, but their questions and answers were dealt with theologically and philosophically, not "scientifically" in the sense of *Religionswissenschaft*. This "scientific" temper in the study of religions developed only at the dawn of the modern period, namely, during the Enlightenment.

Few words are necessary to emphasize the importance of the fifteenth and sixteenth centuries, when the intellectual climate of Europe changed with the discovery of the non-European world. Knowledge of the sacred texts, rituals, and customs of non-European religions gradually became accessible to European intellectuals. Confronted by the diversity of religious phenomena, thinkers like Lord Herbert, Berkeley, Locke, Hume, and

[19] 40:1–2.   [20] 42:1–3.

16

others tried to reconcile the rival claims of religions by digging deeper into the nature of religion itself. The thinkers of the Enlightenment attempted to find the meaning of religion in terms of "reason," rather than depending solely on the authority of "revelation." Locke was hopeful that revelation would confirm the natural knowledge of God given by reason. Hume sought the meaning of religion in its origin, as evidenced in his book, *The Natural History of Religion*. Leibniz differentiated between "contingent truths" and "necessary truths" in religions.

The expression *Religionswissenschaft* was first used in 1867 by Max Müller. Like the Enlightenment thinkers, he was concerned with *religio naturalis*, or the original natural religion of reason, and assumed that "truth" was to be found in the most universal essence of religion and not in its particular manifestations. The process of differentiation of the original truth into diverse religions was seen in much the same way as the Old Testament described the origin of different languages in the legend of the Tower of Babel. Significantly, Max Müller's key to the scientific investigation of religions was philology. He and his disciples were hopeful that by studying the development of languages they could arrive at the essence of religion "scientifically." He used the term *Religionswissenschaft* in order to indicate that the new discipline was freed from the philosophy of religion and from theology, even though in actuality his "science of religion," embracing both comparative theology and theoretical theology, was not too different from philosophy of religion. A Dutch historian of religion, C. P. Tiele, also regarded the science of religions as the philosophic part of the investigation of religious phenomena. While Tiele held that philosophic doctrines of belief and dogmatic systems should not be dealt with in the science of religions, nevertheless this discipline remained a philosophy of religion in Tiele's view. Another Dutch scholar, Chantepie de la Saussaye, did not find a qualitative difference between the science of religions and the philosophy and history of religions, here using the term "history of religions" in its narrower sense.

In retrospect it becomes evident that the scientific study of religions was a product of the Enlightenment. In the study of religion the Enlightenment period accepted the deistic notion of reason and rejected the authority of revelation. The Enlightenment thinkers also accepted the concept of *religio naturalis* or

17

a universal religiosity underlying all historic religions which was to be perceived by reason without the aid of revelation.

The rationalism of the Enlightenment was followed by romanticism, in which the doctrine of *religio naturalis* was again foremost. Van der Leeuw provides us with a careful analysis of the impact of the three romantic periods on the scientific study of religions. First, the period of philosophic romanticism "endeavoured to comprehend the significance of the history of religion by regarding specific religious manifestations as symbols of a primordial revelation." Second, the period of romantic philology, while reacting against the unfettered speculation of romanticism, remained romantic "in its desire to comprehend religion as the expression of a universal mode of human thinking." Third, the period of romantic positivism, preoccupied with the principle of development, still accepted religion to be "the voice of humanity." Thus, Chantepie de la Saussaye, for example, "sought to comprehend the objective appearances of religion in the light of subjective processes."[21]

The early historians of religions, notwithstanding their conscious "emancipation" from philosophy, had definite philosophical assumptions, be they rationalistic or romantic, and they dealt with religio-scientific data "philosophically." According to Joachim Wach, Max Scheler was probably the first scholar who made the distinction between philosophy and *Religionswissenschaft*. Following Max Scheler, Wach held that the religio-scientific task must be carried out not "philosophically" or "scientifically" but "religio-scientifically," with its own methodology. While Wach acknowledged the necessary contributions of philosophy to the scientific study of religions, he rightly insisted that the point of departure of *Religionswissenschaft* was the historically given religions.

Obviously the history of religions or *Religionswissenschaft* does not monopolize the study of religions. Normative studies, such as theology and philosophy, and descriptive disciplines, such as sociology, anthropology, and others, are concerned with various aspects of religions and religious phenomena. At the same time it must be made clear that the history of religions is not merely a collective title for a number of related studies, such

[21] Gerardus van der Leeuw, *Religion in Essence and Manifestation*, trans. J. E. Turner (London: George Allen & Unwin, Ltd., 1938), pp. 691–94.

18

as the history of Islam, Christianity, Buddhism, Hinduism, and primitive religion, or the comparative studies of doctrines, practices, and ecclesiastical institutions of various religions. In short, the history of religions is neither a normative discipline nor solely a descriptive discipline, even though it is related to both.

Our thesis is that the discipline of *Religionswissenschaft* lies between the normative disciplines on the one hand and the descriptive disciplines on the other. Following Wach, we may divide *Religionswissenschaft* into historical and systematic subdivisions. Under the heading of "historical" come the general history of religion and the histories of specific religions. Under the heading of "systematic" come phenomenological, comparative, sociological, and psychological studies of religions. All these subdivisions are regarded as integral parts of *Religionswissenschaft* or the history of religions, in the way we use this term.

While *Religionswissenschaft* is an autonomous discipline in the sense that it is not a composite of various disciplines concerned with the study of religions, it does not claim to be a self-sufficient discipline. That is to say, *Religionswissenschaft* depends heavily on other disciplines, including both normative and descriptive studies of religions. For example, the descriptive aspect of the history of religions must depend on the disciplines which deal with the historical delineation of each religion. Moreover, the analytical aspects of the history of religions must depend on psychology, anthropology, sociology, philosophy, philology, and hermeneutics in its study of various features of religions, such as scriptures, doctrines, cults, and social groupings. This does not mean, however, that *Religionswissenschaft* regards itself as the queen of all disciplines dealing with the study of religions. It simply means that from the standpoint of *Religionswissenschaft* other disciplines can be regarded as its auxiliary disciplines. On the other hand, from the standpoint of a normative or descriptive discipline, *Religionswissenschaft* may be regarded as one of its auxiliary disciplines.

Careful attention must be given to the relation between *Religionswissenschaft* and other disciplines. This is an important question in today's academic world, especially in America. The question of the sociology of religion may be cited as an example of the relation between *Religionswissenschaft* and another discipline. According to Professor E. A. Shils: "It is scarcely to be expected that American sociologists would make contributions to the sociological study of religion along the lines of Max Weber's *Gesammelte Aufsätze zur Religionssoziologie*. American sociologists are usually too poorly educated historically and their religious 'musicality' is too slight to interest themselves in such problems." Nevertheless, Shils cites such works as Kincheloe's *The American City and Its Church*, Niebuhr's *Social Sources of American Denominationalism*, Mecklin's *Story of American Descent*, and Pope's *Millhands and Preachers* as examples of American "sociology of religion."[22] The crucial question arises as to whether the sociology of religion must be viewed as a subdivision of *Religionswissenschaft* or of sociology.

It is our contention that there are two kinds of sociology of religion, one derived from sociology and the other from *Religionswissenschaft*, despite Wach's hope: "We would like to believe that, though there is a Catholic and Marxian philosophy of society, there can be only *one* sociology of religion which we may approach from different angles and realize to a different degree but which would use but one set of criteria."[23] Wach himself defined the task of the sociology of religion as "the investigation of the relation between religion(s) and society in their mutual ways of conditioning each other and also of the configuration of any religiously determined social processes."[24] Throughout his life, Wach tried to bridge the gap between the study of religion and the social sciences from the perspective of *Religionswissenschaft*. In his conclusion of *Sociology of Religion* he states: "The fact that this study is limited to a descriptive sociological examination of religious groups need not be interpreted as an implicit admission that the theological, philosophical, and metaphysical problems and questions growing out of such a study of society have to remain unanswerable. They can and most certainly should be answered."[25] But the sociology of religion as a subdivision of sociology is interested in religion within the frame-

[22] E. A. Shils, "The Present Situation in American Sociology," *Pilot Papers*, II, No. 2 (June, 1947), 23–24.

[23] Wach, "Sociology of Religion," *Twentieth Century Sociology*, ed. G. Gurvitch and W. E. Moore (New York: Philosophical Library, 1945).

[24] Wach, "Religionssoziologie," *Handwörterbuch der Soziologie*, ed. A. Vierkandt, No. 1 (1931), pp. 479–94.

[25] Wach, *Sociology of Religion* (Chicago: University of Chicago Press, 1944), p. 374.

work of the objectives of sociology, that is, "to gain a knowledge of man and society insofar as it may be achieved through investigation of the elements, processes, antecedents and consequences of group living." The sociologist, in his study of the sociology of religion, despite Wach's admonition not to view religion as a function of natural and social groupings and as one form of cultural expression, has to start from the fundamental assumption that "the conduct of the person—his ways of thinking and ways of acting—and the nature of the social order—its structure, function and values—are to be understood as a product of group life."[26] Thus, although both kinds of sociology of religion deal with the same data and may even utilize similar methods, one sociology of religion inevitably views the data "sociologically," whereas the other views the same data "religio-scientifically." Similar observations can be made regarding the relation of *Religionswissenschaft* to other disciplines.

What does it mean to view the data "religio-scientifically"? This is not a simple question. Basically, the point of departure of *Religionswissenschaft* is the historically given religions. In contrast to normative disciplines, *Religionswissenschaft* does not have a speculative purpose, nor can it start from an a priori deductive method. While *Religionswissenschaft* has to be faithful to descriptive principles, its inquiry must nevertheless be directed to the meaning of religious phenomena. Professor Mircea Eliade rightly insists that the meaning of a religious phenomenon can be understood only if it is studied as something religious. "To try to grasp the essence of such a phenomenon by means of physiology, psychology, sociology, economics, linguistics, art or any other study is false; it misses the one unique and irreducible element in it—the element of the sacred."[27] To be sure, Eliade is aware that there are no purely religious phenomena, because no phenomenon can be exclusively religious. But we agree with him that this does not mean that religion can be explained in terms of other functions, such as social, linguistic, or economic. In so stating, however, the historians of religions confront many serious methodological problems.

[26] Philip M. Hauser, "Sociology," *Encyclopaedia Britannica* (1957 ed.).

[27] Mircea Eliade, *Patterns in Comparative Religion*, trans. Rosemary Sheed (New York: Sheed & Ward, 1958), p. xi.

21

IV

One of the fundamental problems confronting the history of religions is that traditional Western scholarship in the field of *Religionswissenschaft* has been too "European" and "Western" in basic orientation and framework. There are two implications of this problem. First, *Religionswissenschaft*, if it is to remain and grow as a religio-scientific inquiry of religions, has to re-examine its methods and categories of interpretation in the light of the criticisms of non-Western scholars in the field. Second, American historians of religions must articulate their unique tradition of scholarship so as to make significant contributions to the world-wide co-operative inquiry in the religio-scientific study of religions.

It is apparent that from the time of the Enlightenment *Religionswissenschaft* has been operating with Western categories in the study of all religions of the world, in spite of its avowed principles of neutrality and objectivity. We know, however, that world religions are developmental movements grounded in historic communities. Thus, the ultimate assumptions of each religion have been colored by decisions of human communities in particular historical and cultural situations. Yet the ultimate assumptions of each religion must be subjected to critical analysis if there is to be any *Wissenschaft* at all. The difficulty is that the assumptions and methodology of *Religionswissenschaft* are also products of Western historical culture. There is no denying that in practice the history of religions has acted too often as though there were such an objective frame of reference. Even those concerned with Eastern religions have asked, unconsciously if not consciously, "Western" questions and have expected Easterners to structure their religions in a way which was meaningful to Westerners. Admittedly, the Eastern emphasis on an immediate apprehension of the totality or essence of Ultimate Reality has been also conditioned by the Eastern historical communities. But the fact remains that the Western historians of religions, with their preoccupation with "conceptualization," have tended to interpret non-Western religious phenomena and attempted to fit them into their logical non-regional abstract systems of *Religionswissenschaft*.

The difference of outlook between Eastern and Western historians of religions seems to be magnified as time goes on in regard to the methodology, aim, and scope of the discipline. Historically, it was the Western scholars who discovered Eastern religions as the subject matters of academic discipline. They too were credited for the training of many Eastern scholars in Western universities. These European-trained Eastern historians of religions, upon returning to their native countries, faced precarious situations.

In the nineteenth century people in the East, under the strong impact of the West and modernity, reacted against the West in several ways. There was a small minority of those who, in their enthusiasm for everything the West stood for, became "denationalized" for all practical purposes. On the other hand, there was another minority who, looking back to their own religious and cultural traditions with a newly acquired Western-type national consciousness, became extremely conservative and rejected the West *in toto*. In this situation, those European-trained Eastern historians of religions became suspect to the conservative elements in the East because of their emphasis on "Western scientific methodology" in the study of traditional religions. At the same time, these newly trained scholars "discovered" afresh the meaning of the Eastern religions; consequently, they were not welcomed by the progressive people who rejected everything traditional. In fact, it took some time for the history of religions to become an accepted discipline in the East. In the course of time, Eastern historians of religions began to reconcile their Western scientific methodology and Eastern world view.

The Eastern attitude, borrowing Dr. Radhakrishnan's oft-repeated expression, may be characterized by the statement, "religion is not a creed or code but an insight into reality." Religion is understood as the life of the inner spirit, available anywhere and everywhere in the universe. Easterners are inclined to feel that religious truth is the sum total of all the religions of the world. This Eastern attitude and understanding of religions enables us to appreciate why the first- and second-generation disciples of Max Müller in Asia were such enthusiastic advocates of the World Parliament of Religions and similar endeavors, and why some of them, such as Radhakrishnan and Anesaki, found their way into the International Committee of Intellectual Cooperation of the League of Nations, and later into UNESCO.

On the other hand, Western historians of religions implicitly feel that religion is not the sum-total of all religions, but rather that "religion" underlies all religions. A religion is thus understood as the particular expression of a universal mode of human reaction to Ultimate Reality. Even today, in the Western tradition of *Religionswissenschaft,* there is an undertone of a search for "universals in religion" or "pure religion" underlying all the empirical manifestations in various religions of the world. Characteristically, many Western historians of religions often suspect the Eastern cosmological outlook as "mystical or intuitive," and not worthy of systematic investigation. On the other hand, the Eastern scholars are becoming critical of the Western scholarship in the field. For example, Dr. D. T. Suzuki observes: "Formerly Buddhists were glad to welcome a scientific approach to their religion. But nowadays a reaction seems to have taken place among them. Instead of relying on scientific arguments for the rationalization of the Buddhist experience they are at present trying to resort to its own dialectics."[28] It might be added that such a development in the East has something in common with the Western development of a "theological history of religions."[29]

In the American setting, it is our fond hope that there will develop several centers of learning in the field of the history of religions. The European centers of learning, nearly all of which were affected by two world wars, continue to devote great interest to this discipline. But the practical difficulties under which they have to work place an increasing responsibility upon American scholarship and initiative. It is encouraging to note that since World War II facilities for the study of Eastern languages, histories, and cultures have been greatly expanded in the United States, but provisions for the study of Eastern religions are still far from adequate. The crucial problem is how to develop coordination and co-operation among (*a*) theoreticians of the systematic aspects of the general history of religions, (*b*) historians of religions who deal with regional cultures and specific religions, (*c*) historians of religions who are competent in auxiliary disciplines, as well as scholars in the related subjects. From this point

[28] Quoted in *Modern Trends in World-Religions,* ed. A. Eustace Haydon (Chicago: University of Chicago Press, 1934), p. 38.

[29] Cf. Joseph M. Kitagawa, "Theology and the Science of Religion," *Anglican Theological Review,* Vol. XXXIX, No. 1 (January, 1957).

of view the introductory address on "The Actual Situation of the History of Religions" by Van der Leeuw at the Seventh Congress for the History of Religions, held in 1950 at Amsterdam, is significant. In it he stressed two main tasks of the history of religions for the future: (1) the need of a friendly relationship between the history of religions and theology and (2) the importance of contacts with other branches of learning, such as philosophy, archeology, anthropology, psychology, and sociology.[30] His statement is particularly pertinent to the American situation. Furthermore, American scholars in the field are in a strategic position to mediate between European and Asiatic schools of thought.

In a comprehensive discipline such as *Religionswissenschaft*, communication among the scholars in the various subdivisions of the field does not develop automatically. For example, the historians of religions who are engaged in the religio-scientific inquiry into Buddhism or Hinduism tend to be preoccupied with their subject matters and do not always relate their findings to the generalists in the field. They would rather work with Buddhologists or Indologists who have little interest in *Religionswissenschaft* as such. In reality, these specialists or those historians of religions engaged in the study of regional cultures or specific religions need informed criticisms both from, say, Buddhologists or Indologists, and from generalists in the field.

It is our observation that in the past both generalists and specialists have tended to be sharply split between inquiries into the theoretical or doctrinal aspects and the historical, phenomenological, institutional, or cultic aspects. It goes without saying that both aspects are important, but what is more important is the study of interplay between theoretical, practical, and sociological aspects of religions. In order to understand the history of a specific religion integrally and religio-scientifically, one cannot ignore the problem of its origin, which, incidentally, fascinated the historians of religions of the nineteenth century. However, one must remember the admonition of Tor Andrae that the origin of religion is not a historical question; ultimately it is a metaphysical one. Thus, the popular theories of *Urmonotheismus* or high-god, interesting though they may be, cannot be used as

[30] *Proceedings of the Seventh Congress for the History of Religions* (Amsterdam: North-Holland Publishing Co., 1951), p. 20.

the basis of the religio-scientific study of religions with utmost certainty. What is probably most meaningful and fruitful is an approach toward a historic religion as a "wholeness." This task, however, is not an easy one. As a working hypothesis, we agree with Professor Gibb that Islam, or any other religion for that matter, "is an autonomous expression of religious thought and experience, which must be viewed in and through itself and its own principles and standards."[31] In order to follow this principle, one must study the historical development of a religion, in itself and in interaction with the culture and society. One must try to understand the emotional make-up of the religious community and its reaction or relation to the outside world. Finally, there must be added a religio-sociological analysis, in our sense of the term, the aim of which is to analyze the social background, to describe the structure, and to ascertain the sociologically relevant implications of the religious movement and institutions. One must be sensitive throughout to the internal consistency of the various aspects of the religious community. This is indeed a difficult task.

The term "internal consistency" is used advisedly in order to get away from popularly accepted genetic, causal theories, such as that Buddha rebelled against Brahmanism, therefore Buddhism rejects the caste system. Unfortunately, the field of the history of religions is plagued by many such dangerous oversimplifications. The pioneers in the field were largely responsible for this. Many of them had definite ideas about the so-called essence of each religion, such as its concepts of deity, of the nature and destiny of man and of the world, which have been handed down to us through manuals and handbooks that are abundant in the European tradition of *Religionswissenschaft*. These shorter treatises are useful and instructive, especially on the introductory level, but they must be used with great care. It is dangerous to explain, for instance, all the cultic and sociological features of Islam solely in terms of the religious experience of Muhammad. There is a gap between ideals and actual practices in all religions. At the same time, what is happening in remote villages in Turkey or Indonesia cannot be under-

---

[31] Sir Hamilton A. R. Gibb, *Mohammedanism, an Historical Survey* ("Home University Library" ed. [London, 1953]), p. vii.

26

stood without some reference to the life and teaching of Muhammad. Such is the problem of internal consistency.

Let us take another example. What does it mean when we say that the Vedas are central in Hinduism? If we accept the religious authority of the Vedic literature in the orthodox schools, we must also be aware of the fact that the Vedas have been interpreted, modified, believed, and abused by men throughout the ages. Or we may study the sacrificial system of Hinduism, but that again is not all of Hinduism. How, then, can we possibly understand the internal consistency despite these seeming contradictions which characterize historic and contemporary Hinduism? And yet, all aspects of Hinduism—theoretic, cultic, and sociological—are held together, and they are closely related to arts, literature, customs, politics, economics, and other aspects of Hindu history and culture. The task of the historian of religion is to try to feel and understand the "adhesiveness" of various aspects of historic religions.

But can we understand the adhesiveness and internal consistencies of religions and cultures other than our own? Here is the crux of the problem for the historian of religions. It is small comfort to know that other scholars, such as those who deal with intellectual history, confront similar difficulties.[32] The historians of religions, in order to understand other religions of various cultural areas and historic epochs, must think of themselves as observers and investigators. Their own assumptions inevitably prevent them from entering into the inner world of other peoples, to say nothing of the difficulties involved in the linguistic and cultural gap. Often, written records must be checked by oral traditions and "acted myths." Language is dynamic; it is always changing. It influences the culture, but men's thinking and experience also influence language. It is impossible to abstract such words as *moksha* and *nirvana* from the historical contexts of ancient and modern India, China, Burma, and Japan and expect these words to have the same connotations.

The religious commitment, or lack of commitment, of a historian of religions must also be taken into account. Regardless of his formal affiliation with any ecclesiastical institution or adherence

[32] John K. Fairbank (ed.), "Introduction: Problems of Method and of Content," *Chinese Thought and Institutions* (Chicago: University of Chicago Press, 1957).

to a faith, he is never free from commitments on various issues, partly because of his upbringing and partly because of his fundamental decisions about life. In the words of Professor Benjamin Schwartz: "While these commitments are bound to color his understanding to some extent, he can make an effort to distinguish in his own mind between his commitments and his attempts to understand the conscious response of others. On the other hand, the illusion of complete non-involvement, with all the self-deceptions it nourishes, is more detrimental to objectivity than a lively sense of involvement controlled by the desire to understand."[33]

One's religious faith is both an advantage and a disadvantage in the religio-scientific inquiry. It is true that "the only and the best way to learn how to pray is to pray." We may recall Professor Hocking's account of Jesuits in Kurseong, who are "poised, unhurried, with firm judgment and far vision," dedicated to the study of the religions of India. More often than not, however, those who study other religions with firm conviction about their own faith are what Hocking calls "partly prepared men." He says: "It is as though the graduate level of adept preparation were out of tune with our sense of haste and scantiness of means. . . . The real lack . . . is a lack of perception; a certain triviality . . . a supposition that we already know enough, and that more thinking is a luxury that can be dispensed with."[34] Furthermore, it must be kept in mind that the historian of religions is engaged in the religio-scientific inquiry of religions for the sake of "understanding," and not for the service of the propagation of any particular faith. While we recognize the important role of a "theological history of religions," this is a theological discipline, and we must maintain a wholesome tension between the history of religions and a theological history of religions.[35]

Nevertheless, the religio-scientific inquiry of a historic religion cannot stop there. Any religion is man's experience of, response and commitment to, Ultimate Reality in a specific historic situation. No religion, however regional and ethnocentric,

[33] Benjamin Schwartz, "The Intellectual History of China," in Fairbank, *op. cit.*, p. 74.

[34] William Ernest Hocking, *Living Religions and a World Faith* (New York: Macmillan Co., 1940), pp. 206–7.

[35] Kitagawa, "The Nature and Program of the History of Religions Field," *Divinity School News*, November, 1957.

28

can be interpreted without reference to universal human themes, such as birth, death, love, marriage, frustration, meaningless-ness, and beatific vision. Just as in intellectual history, the re-ligio-scientific inquiry has to proceed in the manner of oscilla-tion between the universal religious themes and particular re-ligious systems, communities, and histories, because all religions, both lofty and superstitious, are integral parts of the universal history of religions. Even for the sake of under-standing one specific religion, we must relate it to the larger framework. As Fairbank suggests, "each step in such an oscillation leads into problems," such as the problems of a text or a historic figure. "Inevitably we are faced with the broad question of the cultural circumstances, the social insti-tutions and events. . . . In this stage of our process there is no logical stopping place short of the total historical comprehension of human history on earth; we must use our understanding of the whole historical process, such as it may be."[36] Here we enter the most difficult stage of the *Allgemeine Religionswissenschaft.* "It is less difficult to amass factual data, on the one hand, and to understand generalized concepts, on the other, than to fit them all together in an integrated, articulate account."[37] Ulti-mately, such a synthetic systematization must depend on many years of research and the genius of individual scholars, whereas individual scholars must be engaged constantly in the co-opera-tive inquiry with like-minded scholars, who can provide them with informed criticisms, insights, and suggestions.

We discussed earlier some aspects of the problems of teaching the history of religions in colleges, universities, and seminaries in America. Questions have been raised again and again as to the real significance of the history of religions. The answer is to be found, in part at least, in the aim of education itself. We agree with John Henry Newman, who held that the object of a uni-versity is intellectual and not moral, and we might paraphrase him by saying that the significance of the teaching of the history of religions must be intellectual and not "religious" in the tra-ditional sense of the term.

This essay was written with the conviction that the curricu-lums of all institutions of higher learning should include courses in the religio-scientific study of a variety of religions, including

[36] *Op. cit.,* pp. 4–5.   [37] *Ibid.,* p. 5.

29

some of the major religions of the East as well as the Judeo-Christian religious traditions of the West. While many institutions are consciously attempting to present alternative interpretations of significant religious and philosophical questions in the Western tradition, a surprising number of leading schools in America have as yet done nothing to acquaint their students with the questions which have been raised in the non-Western religious and cultural traditions. We are not advocating that all students must become experts in *Religionswissenschaft*. But certainly in this bewildered world of our time, students ought to be exposed to some of the deepest issues of life, as they have been experienced and understood by the noblest men and women through the ages, in the East as well as in the West.

The history of religions, if it is taught competently in the undergraduate colleges, universities, and seminaries, can widen the intellectual and spiritual horizons of students by bringing to them these deeper dimensions of life and culture in the dreams and faith by which men live.

WILFRED CANTWELL SMITH

Comparative Religion: Whither—and Why?

The thirteen-volume *Encyclopaedia of Religion and Ethics*, (1908–21, and recently reissued) is an impressive work.[1] Not only does it serve as a great warehouse of information, indispensable to all careful students of the world's religious history. More than that, it may be taken also as a symbol. I see it as typifying a culmination of the first great stage of scholarship in this field: the accumulation, organization, and analysis of facts.[2] This stage began, one may say, with the Age of Discovery, when Western Christendom reached out to the rest of the world, probing, exploring, gradually becoming aware of peoples and places far beyond its erstwhile horizon. There were brought back accounts, weird or wonderful, of other men's religions—at first haphazardly, as travelers' tales, later in more ordered fashion and more

[1] *The Encyclopaedia of Religion and Ethics*, ed. James Hastings, with the assistance of John A. Selbie . . . and Louis H. Gray (Edinburgh, 1908–21; New York, 1955).

[2] I hope that I may be forgiven for using the first person singular in this article, when expressing my own views, in place of the more conventional and less stark editorial "we." I have been pushed into doing so by the fact that a good part of the argument in this essay turns on the use of pronouns; and I am particularly concerned to note how the word "we" is used religiously and by scholars of religion. I have therefore avoided using it here myself so far as possible (I resort to it only when I mean myself and my readers—presumably fellow students of comparative religion in one way or another—or when I mean mankind, including my readers and myself).

31

abundantly. The nineteenth century saw the rise of a great attempt to give this matter serious and disciplined consideration: searching out material, recording it carefully, scrutinizing it systematically, interpreting it. This was the task of the universities, which gradually enshrined oriental studies and anthropological studies and here and there established chairs of *Religionswissenschaft*.

In our day a new development in these studies is to be discerned, inaugurating a second major stage, of rather different type. In suggesting this, I do not mean that the first phase is finished. It continues, and will continue. Information of increasing breadth and increasing precision, analyses of increasing complexity, presentations of increasing erudition and subtlety, must and will go on. I would hold, however, that these things, while not superseded, are being now transcended. The exciting new frontiers of inquiry and of challenge lie at a new and higher level.

In the first phase there was amassed an imposing knowledge about other peoples' religions. In the second phase it is those other peoples themselves that are present. The large-scale compilation of data of the nineteenth century and up to World War I has in the twentieth century and particularly since World War II been supplemented by a living encounter—a large-scale face-to-face meeting between persons of diverse faith.

In a sense, the modern counterpart to the *Encyclopaedia* are such facts as that in 1936 Sir Sarvepalli Radhakrishnan was appointed Spalding Professor of Eastern Thought at Oxford; in 1952 the Institute of Islamic Studies was opened at McGill with half its teaching staff and half its students Muslims; at the present time visiting Buddhist scholars have been invited to the Chicago Divinity School; and so on. Westerners professionally concerned with the Orient, including its religious life, are now expected to visit the communities about which they write, and most do keep in frequent and close personal touch.[3] And just as in medicine a graduate may not practice until he has added an internship to his academic training, so at McGill University it is a formal requirement for the doctorate in Islamic Studies

[3] It is coming to be recognized that part of the cost of setting up a department of oriental studies in a Western university is the provision of travel funds and of arrangements for what is unfortunately still called "leave," for the staff, who must have access to the Orient just as much as a chemistry professor must have access to a chemistry laboratory.

that the candidate "at some stage in his adult life, before, during, or after his work at McGill shall have spent some time (preferably at least two years, and in any case not less than the equivalent of one academic session) in the Islamic world."[4]

Moreover, it is not only professional students that are affected; the general reading or thinking public has also moved into the new phase. When the *Encyclopaedia* was published, intellectuals of Europe and America had available in it and in a series of books information about the "non-Christian"[5] world; today intellectuals and also others find that they personally have Buddhist or Muslim neighbors or colleagues or rivals.

Future historians, it has been said, will look back upon the twentieth century not primarily for its scientific achievements but as the century of the coming-together of peoples, when all mankind for the first time became one community.

That this situation is of political, social, and cultural significance is evident enough. But is it also of academic import? Is the comparative study of religion thereby changed or even affected? It becomes more urgent and more central, certainly. In addition, I am suggesting, there is inherently involved a major modification in the nature and the manner of our work. And I believe that this second great development is a change for the good: that the personalization of comparative religion studies is transforming them into something more realistic, truer. In this case one cannot suggest any striking achievement as symbol; this stage has not yet culminated in any great work, and indeed it is both so complex and so incipient that neither its importance nor its implications have yet been clearly recognized. Yet it constitutes the basic advance in this field of our day. Our chief challenge is to understand this development and to carry it to a successful conclusion.

The new world situation is compelling us to explore what I might call the essentially human quality of our subject matter.

[4] From the "Memorandum on the Ph.D. in Islamic Studies," Institute of Islamic Studies, July, 1957.

[5] This term is used advisably here, to designate the nineteenth-century attitude. As a matter of fact, I would suggest that there is hardly a more fruitful way towards misunderstanding a Muslim, a Hindu, or a Buddhist than that of thinking of him as a "non-Christian." By the use of such negative concepts it is possible to miss altogether the positive quality of another's faith.

If we can effectively come to grips with this, we shall have taken a very considerable step forward towards doing justice to the study that we have ventured to take on. But it is not easy. The implications are many and subtle. Religion being what it is, and man being what he is, the task of adequately conceptualizing the personalization that is today involved will demand our best efforts, of careful scholarship and creative thinking.

The present essay is an exploratory attempt to delineate and to analyse trends and to urge desiderata.

The argument may be summarized briefly, in pronominal terms. The traditional form of Western scholarship in the study of other men's religion was that of an impersonal presentation of an "it." The first great innovation in recent times has been the personalization of the faiths observed, so that one finds a discussion of a "they." Presently the observer becomes personally involved, so that the situation is one of a "we" talking about a "they." The next step is a dialogue, where "we" talk to "you." If there is listening and mutuality, this may become that "we" talk *with* "you." The culmination of this progress is when "we all" are talking *with* each other about "us."

Let me elaborate this.

I

The first and altogether fundamental step has been the gradual recognition of what was always true in principle, but was not always grasped: that the study of a religion is the study of persons. Of all branches of human inquiry, hardly any deals with an area so personal as this. Faith is a quality of men's lives. "All religions are new religions, every morning. For religions do not exist up in the sky somehwere, elaborated, finished, and static; they exist in men's hearts."[6]

We are studying, then, something not directly observable. Let us be quite clear about this, and bold. Personally, I believe this

[6] As will become clear as the argument proceeds, I am not subscribing to that type of humanism that asserts that religious faith amounts to no more than a projection of human hopes, aspirations, and the like. What I am contending is that the *study* of religious faith, and especially of the faith of persons belonging to a tradition other than one's own, must be a study not only of tangible externals but of human hopes and aspirations and interpretations of those externals. The quotation is from my earlier essay, "The Comparative Study of Religion: Reflections on the Possibility and Purpose of a Religious Science," *McGill University, Faculty of Divinity, Inaugural Lectures* (Montreal, 1950), p. 51.

to be true finally of all work in the humanities, and believe that we should not be plaintive about it or try somehow to circumvent it. It is our glory that we study not things but qualities of personal living. This may make our work more difficult than that of the scientists but it makes it also more important, and in a significant sense more true. Ideas, ideals, loyalties, passions, aspirations cannot be directly observed, but their role in human history is not the less consequential, nor their study less significant or valid.[7] Nor do the transcendent matters to which these may, no doubt inadequately, refer, have a status in the universe the less solid. A galaxy may be larger, but a value I hold to be not only more important but at least equally real and in some ways more real.[8]

A fundamental error of the social sciences, and a fundamental lapse even of some humanists, has been to take the observable manifestations of some human concern as if they were the concern itself. The proper study of mankind is by inference.

The externals of religion—symbols, institutions, doctrines, practices—can be examined separately; and this is largely what in fact was happening until quite recently, perhaps particularly in European scholarship. But these things are not in themselves religion, which lies rather in the area of what these mean to those that are involved. The student is making effective progress when he recognizes that he has to do not with religious systems basically but with religious persons; or at least, with something interior to persons.

Certainly there has been and remains a great deal of preliminary work to be done in the realm of tangible data, of what I have called the externals of religion. It is only as these are accurately established, that the study of the religions themselves can proceed; and this latter must continually be revised as the former become more exactly known. It is not a crucial question whether the same scholars do both tasks or whether there is division of labor. Nor is it worth quarreling about the relative value of the two; both are needed. What one would advocate is

[7] On the study of unobservables in human behavior, cf. my *Islam in Modern History* (Princeton, 1957), pp. 7, n. 4, 8, n. 5.

[8] One wonders if a case should not be made for reviving the once lucid and important notion that there may be gradations of reality. For long it has been assumed that something is either real or unreal, with no room for a possibility of intermediate degrees.

clarity. The time has come when those in this field must recognize to what extent an article or a book or a conference or a committee is concerned with the externals of the history of the religion and to what extent with the history of the religions themselves. I am also suggesting that over the past century there has been, and am guessing that in the near future there will increasingly be, a development in the direction of more awareness that religions are human involvements.

The point may be illustrated widely. When in 1934 Archer published a general textbook, *Faiths Men Live By*,[9] the title was arresting. The nineteenth-century scholar did not think in such terms, though today the attitude is almost standard. The striking works of Pratt, *India and Its Faiths* (1915) and *A Pilgrimage of Buddhism* (1928) did much to make these religions come alive for the first time for many Western readers; for Pratt had a gift not only of brilliance but of extraordinary human sympathy.[10] These are clear instances of the increasing mobility of modern man: each book was written as the result of travel in the East. Personalization can be achieved also, however, in the case of the religion of an historical community that has ceased to exist: Frankfort's recent *Ancient Egyptian Religion*[11] differs from the first Western monograph, by Erman,[12] some forty years earlier, in considerable part as a study of people over against a study of data.[13]

[9] John Clark Archer, *Faiths Men Live By* (New York, 1934). There have been several subsequent editions. The earlier, popular work, Lewis Browne, *This Believing World* (New York, 1928), made the same point; and there were others.

[10] James Bissett Pratt, *India and Its Faiths: A Traveler's Record* (Boston and New York, 1915); *A Pilgrimage of Buddhism and a Buddhist Pilgrimage* (New York, 1928). That Pratt was conscious that he was doing something new in this realm is clear from his Preface, though I feel that he was not quite clear as to what it was. It was his interest in psychology, and his lack of training in oriental classics, that gave him his personalist approach.

[11] H. Frankfort, *Ancient Egyptian Religion: An Interpretation* (New York, 1948).

[12] Adolf Erman, *Die Religion der alten Aegypter* (Berlin, 1905).

[13] Frankfort also is conscious that he is innovating, and he states the point almost in the terms of my present argument: "Erman . . . gave . . . a masterly but patronizing account of weird myth, doctrines, and usages, while the peculiarly religious values which these contained remained hidden from his lucid rationalism. . . . Since then . . . the most prolific writers . . . assumed towards our subject a scientist's rather than a scholar's attitude: while ostensibly concerned with religion, they were really absorbed in the

Perhaps one should say, with more precision, the study of a people's religious life over against a study of their gods, their doctrines, their institutions, and the like. The difference is in attitude and treatment. We must repeat, perhaps, that there continues to be a need for scholarly work on the externals. Erman's study fails not because it deals with these (he was an important Egyptologist) but because it makes the mistake of presenting these as the religion itself. Our plea would be that from now on any study of externalia recognize itself as such; that only those deserve to be accepted as studies of religion that do justice to the fact that they deal with the life of men.

Part of the personalization of our studies is evinced in the shift over past decades to a primary interest in the major living religions of the world. (The phrase "living religions," which has become current, is itself significant.)[14] Whereas at the turn of the century a typical introductory course in this field would emphasize "primitive religions," and a typical book would address itself to "the nature and origin of religion" (the phrase implicitly postulates that the reality or truth of religion is to be found most purely or most surely in its earliest and simplest forms), today it is normal to give chief or even sole attention to Hindus, Buddhists, and Muslims, along with Christians and Jews—groups that between them constitute the vast majority of today's population,[15] and between them claim most forcefully

---

task of bringing order to a confused mass of material. Men of this school have dominated this subject for the last twenty or thirty years; they possess a splendid knowledge of the texts and have enriched our information greatly. But in reading their books you would never think that the gods they discuss once moved men to acts of worship" (Preface, pp. v–vi).

[14] It is the title, for instance, of a recent work: Frederic Spiegelberg, *Living Religions of the World* (Englewood Cliffs, N.J., 1956); and of various others. It is to be found also nowadays as the title of course offerings in college curricula. I doubt that one would find it academically as title of either book or course at the turn of the century.

[15] Many examples could be given. One illustrative title is that of Edward J. Jurji (ed.), *The Great Religions of the Modern World* (Princeton, 1946, and several times reprinted). As the wording suggests, this is one of those volumes that omit any treatment of "primitives." One example among many of the same point from college curricula is the fact that at the Divinity School, University of Chicago, apart from an introductory course on analytic principles, there is one basic ("Common-Core") course in this field, "Contemporary World Religions" (HR 302; in the 1957–58 and 1958–59 *An-*

to represent religion's highest and truest development. And whereas once such attention as was given to the great religions was primarily to their scriptures and historically to their early, classical phases, today these religions are seen primarily as the faith of present-day groups.[16]

In the case of the living religions this matter affects not only the conception of what is being studied, but also the method employed. First, there is an important epistemological point. In the study of a religion other than one's own, a knowledge of its institutions, formulations, and overt history may be derived from things. But if they are seen as clues to a personal quality of men's lives, then a sympathetic appreciation of this quality may at least in part be derived from having adherents of that faith as

---

nouncements). Until recently a specializing student could elect a course on primitive religions, in advanced work, though even there this took a minor place alongside studies of the more advanced great faiths—especially Buddhism, on which Chicago has been concentrating. And even this has now been dropped, apparently in favor of a new course, on Christian and Western positions vis-à-vis the other world religions (cf. HR 341 in the 1957–58 *Announcements* with HR 342 in that for 1958–59)—a shift towards a "we/they" orientation that we consider in our next section. The same omission of primitives and concern for the great religions is true of the recent brilliant text of Huston Smith, *The Religions of Man* (New York, 1958)—this last is a luminous example of the treatment of religion as the faith of *persons:* note the opening paragraphs, which present people worshiping, the book moving on from this to portray their religion as the substance of their worshiping. Note also the opening pages of other chapters. This book, indeed, virtually recognizes, or at least confirms, the point that I am making in this present essay, for the author explicitly states in his Preface that the reader should turn to other (earlier) books for the data of the religions, while he is moving on from these to proffer an interpretation of those data (cf. his note 1 to chap. i, p. 315). This work is perhaps the first adequate textbook in world religions, precisely because it treats religions as human.

[16] Note the Chicago course offering and the Smith book mentioned in the preceding note. At a more popular level one may instance the series in various issues of *Life* magazine (New York, 1955), later republished independently as a book, *The World's Great Religions* (New York, 1957). (A Dutch version has also appeared: *De grote Gotsdiensten der Wereld* [1958].) Significantly, the Introduction is entitled "How Mankind Worships" (by Paul Hutchinson), pp. 1–8.

Furthermore, Harvard University, inaugurating in 1958 a new program in this field, chose to name it neither History of Religion(s) nor Comparative Religion, which for some decades have shared the field between them, but "Program in World Religions."

informants[17] and perhaps even as friends.[18] Of the various ways of finding out what something means to the person concerned, one way is to ask him.

[17] An illustrative development has been the publication for Western students of the Morgan series on comparative religion, in which Hindus, Buddhists, and Muslims present their own faiths: Kenneth W. Morgan (ed.), *The Religion of the Hindus* (New York, 1953); *The Path of the Buddha: Buddhism Interpreted by Buddhists* (New York, 1956); *Islam—the Straight Path: Islam Interpreted by Muslims* (New York, 1958). There are many other examples of the growing recognition in the West that to understand an alien religion one should allow its adherents to speak for themselves. One is the 1952 paperback publication of the Qur'an explicitly in a Muslim's translation (*The Meaning of the Glorious Koran: An Explanatory Translation by Mohammed Marmaduke Pickthall* [New York: Mentor Books, 1953]—note the opening sentence of the Foreword: "The aim of this work is to present to English readers what Muslims of the world over hold to be the meaning of the words of the Koran. . . . It may be reasonably claimed that no Holy Scripture can be fairly presented by one who disbelieves its inspiration and its message"). Another is the series of London editions of Indian classics with expository commentaries by Radhakrishnan (*The Bhagavadgītā, with an Introductory Essay, Sanskrit Text, English Translation and Notes by S. Radhakrishnan* (London, 1948 and subsequent reprints); *The Principal Upaniṣads, Edited with Introduction, Text, Translation and Notes by S. Radhakrishnan* (London, 1953; etc.); and many more.

[18] The differences are significant in many ways, some of which will be considered below under the heading of "encounter." It is a step forward to recognize that adherents of a religion should speak for that religion. Yet this is not in itself enough. For one thing, it has long been recognized that a faith cannot adequately be expressed in words, not even by a man who holds it devoutly. To understand what is in his heart, therefore, the student must not merely listen to or read what a believer affirms, but must come to know those qualities of the believer's life that can become known only in that personal two-way relationship known as friendship. This is peculiarly true of religious faith, but applies in some measure to all human discourse. It is to misunderstand man not to recognize that the knowledge of a person available to another person depends quite basically on the personal relationship between them. I cannot know my neighbor more than superficially unless I love him. So seriously is it believed at McGill University that a Western student is not being offered adequate facilities for the study of Islam and for a degree in Islamics unless he has Muslims available from whom to learn, that it is formal policy at its Institute of Islamic Studies that half of the teachers and half of the students be Muslims. In the case of a dead religion, such a regulation cannot be administratively established, but the principle is not entirely invalidated: all interpretations of bygone faiths must in principle be tentative, since there is in fact no final way of checking whether an ascribed meaning was in fact operative. The Frankfort reconstruction of ancient Egyptian religion mentioned above has in fact been criticized by other Egyptologists as insufficiently supported by the data. Not being a scholar in this field, I cannot assess the cogency of such charges. I simply insist that what Frankfort was trying to do in his lectures is not merely legit-

There is a further point, concerning the audience of any study. An important question about any book is, for whom—whether consciously or unconsciously—was it written. What gets written is determined in part by the experience of the writer, in part by that of the persons addressed. Here too our novel world situation, where both people and books now move freely across cultural frontiers, has been pushing comparative religion writers towards a greatly increased personalization in what they write. As we have already remarked, the Western reader of a Western book about what used to be exotic religion will increasingly himself have Asian friends, or African experience, or international responsibilities. The consumer pressure for the production of studies about the faiths of others is no longer only academic interest or idle curiosity, but is a demand for an interpretation of people with whom one has to deal.

Moreover, books by Western scholars about, say, Buddhism are increasingly being read by Buddhists. Few Western authors have been conscious of the wide extent to which this has become true. Even fewer have grasped its important implications. I would put forward two propositions, both rather bold and perhaps more in process of becoming cogent than actually valid as yet but, I am persuaded, increasingly important. The first is that it is no longer legitimate to write in this field for any but a world audience. Many think that they are addressing books and articles to one particular community (normally their own), but these are in fact read by others, and especially by that other community that they are about. Muslim writing about the West or about Christianity or Christendom, though in Arabic or Urdu or whatever and produced for Muslim consumption, is being

---

imate but imperative. If he has not done it well, then others must do it better; but we cannot accept the view that it should not be attempted. As historical criticism in literature, art, and other humane studies has long known, there are ways of attempting to reconstruct what was going on in the minds and hearts of people now dead. Such ways can also be resorted to in the case of people now living; but here they can be checked or supplemented by contact with the persons themselves. And even for persons not accessible, I would hold that sympathy plays a part in any human capacity to understand.

I do not suggest that a personalist epistemology is infallible. It is possible to be inadequately informed, and even misinformed. Personal explanations must be checked against or co-ordinated with texts and other overt data. The personalist approach does not replace other methods, but in our present world surely cannot fail to supplement.

40

studied and analysed by Western scholars, and the results published. This has two sets of consequences: a somewhat sensitive awareness of the fact is beginning to be not without its effect on the course of Muslim writing itself, in addition to the effect on Western orientation to Islam.

It is much more widely true that books by Western scholars[19] expounding, let us say, Islam to Westerners, or analysing the rise of Mahayana Buddhism in terms of an academic tradition of secular rationalism, are increasingly studied by those concerned.[20] So far this fact has led to only limited awareness and had very limited effect on the course of such Western writing, but these have begun to be discernible[21] and must increase. The effect on the East has been great, and is growing. Western writing on Eastern religion has had, in the course of the last hundred years, because of its substance, an influence on the development of those religions themselves that certainly deserves careful historical investigation; on the whole, because of the form in which it has mostly been cast, it has in addition been causing resentment and is beginning to elicit protest.[22] Certainly anyone

[19] Also non-scholars, though this concerns us here less directly: a graphic example was the article "The Moslem World" (actually on its religion) in *Time*, August 31, 1951, pp. 32–37, which gave great offense in the Muslim world and resulted in *Time's* being banned for a while in more than one Muslim country.

[20] It has even happened that two industrious researchers in Beirut have combed writings by Christian missionaries discussing the Christian missionary movement to Muslims, and published their ensuing indictment: Muṣṭafá Khālidī wa 'Umar Farrukh, *al-Tabshīr wa al-Istiʿmār fī al-bilād al-ʿArabīyah* (Beirut, 1372/1953).

[21] An instance, that of Montgomery Watt, is pointed out in n. 42.

[22] As one example among many, see Khurshid Ahmed, *Islam and the West* (Lahore, n.d.) (sc. 1958), a Jamāʿat-i Islāmī pamphlet. (Though ostensibly addressed to the West, this work—which deserves a very careful study—was in fact aimed also at those Westernizing young Muslims who seemed to the author to be in danger of being too much influenced in their own religious ideas by Western writing on Islam.) The increasingly expressed dissatisfaction among Muslims at the otherwise impressive work of European scholarship, *The Encyclopaedia of Islâm* (Leiden and London, 1908–38, and currently being reissued in revised form, Leiden and London, 1954–), is in part to be included also under this present heading. In addition, however, it is in part rather an indication of the resentment of a people inchoately feeling themselves excluded from a conversation about their own affairs. The protests led the editors to recognize self-consciously for the first time that the encyclopedia was in fact produced not for men in general but specifically for (as well as by) the scholarly tradition of Western Europe. This sort of situation is discussed in my next section, below.

for whom comparative religion studies are something that might or should serve to promote mutual understanding and good relations between religious communities cannot but be concerned at this contrary effect. Even by those to whom this is a moral point not essentially germane to the intellectual principles involved, it may yet be recognized that a situation has arisen wherein anyone who writes about a religion other than his own today does so, in effect, in the presence of those about whom he is speaking.

If nothing more, an author not alert to the point that we have been urging, namely, that a religion is a personal thing in the lives of men, is today being alerted to it by the increasingly live reaction to his writing of those men themselves.

As it becomes more widely recognized that the comparative religionist speaks in the hearing of those he describes, this will inescapably have its effect at least on how things are put and perhaps also on the kind of thing said. The point is that an author must write not only more courteously but more responsibly.

I would contend that not only is such a development taking place but that it ought to take place, deliberately and rapidly. For I would proffer this as my second proposition: that no statement about a religion is valid unless it can be acknowledged by that religion's believers. I know that this is revolutionary, and I know that it will not be readily conceded; but I believe it to be profoundly true and important. It would take a good deal more space than is here available to defend it at length; for I am conscious of many ways in which it can be misunderstood and of many objections that can be brought against it which can be answered only at some length. I will only recall that by "religion" here I mean as previously indicated the faith in men's hearts. On the external data about religion, of course, an outsider can by diligent scholarship discover things that an insider does not know and may not be willing to accept. But about the meaning that the system has for those of faith, an outsider cannot in the nature of the case go beyond the believer; for their piety *is* the faith, and if they cannot recognize his portrayal, then it is not their faith that he is portraying. There are complications regarding historical change; I recognize that a religion develops, whereas few believers do recognize this,[23] so that

[23] I have studied some of the intricacies of the notion of a religion's developing, in my Inaugural Lecture mentioned in note 6, above.

42

what once was true about it may no longer be so, and the insider can speak authoritatively only for the present.[24] There are other complications too. All of these must be taken into account in any final exposition; some of them have been explored, others need further clarification. But on the fundamental point I have no qualms: I would hold emphatically that fruitful study must recognize this principle. Indeed, it is not really a limitation but a creative principle; for it provides experimental control that can lead a student dynamically towards the truth.[25]

Non-Christians might write an authoritative history of the church but however clever, erudite, or wise they can never refute Christians on what the Christian faith is. The only way that outsiders can ever ascertain what Christianity is, is by inference from Christian work or art or deed; and they can never be better qualified than those Christians to judge whether their inferences are valid. Indeed, some Christians have maintained that in principle no one can understand Christianity who does not accept it. We do not go so far, but we recognize substance in this contention. We recognize also that a similar point applies to all religions. Anything that I say about Islam as a living faith is valid only in so far as Muslims can say "amen" to it.

The reverse is certainly not true. Not every statement about Islam that is acceptable to Muslims is *ipso facto* true: one can flatter or beguile. Nor need outsiders simply follow Muslims: It is possible both in theory and in practice for an outside scholar to break new ground in stating the meaning of a faith in, say, modern terms more successfully than a believer. At the present time, for instance, Muslims themselves have not been able to give an intellectual statement of their faith that succeeds well

[24] And with final authority only for himself. The subtle question of the relation of one man's faith to his community's faith I am examining in a series of forthcoming lectures on the history of the concept "Religion."

[25] For instance, Huston Smith, in the book to which reference has been made (above, n. 15), states in his Preface that he has had scholarly members of the faiths concerned read some of his chapters. This, which has ceased to be surprising, implicitly supports the principle for validity that I have formulated, as well as showing how the procedure can be productive. Again, the publishers proclaim on the dust-jacket of another recent work (Edmund Perry, *The Gospel in Dispute* [see n. 34, below], the publishers are Doubleday): "Dr. Perry has used the skills of the cultural anthropologist in presenting a clear picture of the four leading non-Christian religions—a picture accepted enthusiastically by their exponents." Even making allowances for commercial overstatement, one may find the claim interesting, suggesting what the publishers expect readers nowadays to approve.

43

in communicating meaning to a Western audience.[26] The task of a non-Muslim scholar writing about Islam is that of constructing an exposition that will do justice to the Western academic tradition, by growing directly out of the objective evidence and by being rationally coherent both within itself and with all other knowledge, and at the same time will do justice to the faith in men's hearts by commanding their assent once it is formulated. It is a creative task and a challenging one.[27]

Whether or not this particular argument carries full conviction, we pass on. The general point that has been made is that in the new conditions of the modern world the comparative study of religion has moved into a new phase—first, in that the object of inquiry has on a quite new scale been seen to be communities of persons. Enough has been said to emphasize the point that the implications of this development are far from negligible.

II

Our second point is that the subject of inquiry also has been taking on a personalized quality: the investigator. Formerly the scholar was seen, ideally, as the detached academic intellect, surveying its material impersonally, almost majestically, and reporting on it objectively. Such a concept is characteristic of the academic tradition of Western Europe; one might be bold enough to add, characteristic particularly of nineteenth-century Western Europe. One cannot belittle that tradition or its accomplishments, in our field or in others. Yet in three ways the situation has become more complex since.

First, the detachment was felt in this particular case to mean,

[26] It has been recognized, even by some Muslims (in private conversation), that Part I of Kenneth Cragg, *The Call of the Minaret* (New York and London, 1956), is a more effective exposition of Islam to Christians than any modern Muslim has been able to accomplish. Compare also my review of Morgan (ed.), *Islam—the Straight Path: Islam Interpreted by Muslims*, in *Journal of the American Oriental Society*, 1959.

[27] My recent *Islam in Modern History* (Princeton, 1957) was a deliberate and explicit attempt to meet this challenge; see the Preface, pp. v–x. Particularly relevant here is the attempted exposition of the meaning of Islam as a religion, pp. 9–26. The book was deliberately written in an endeavor to be simultaneously (1) true (and intelligible, cogent, to academic scholars), (2) intelligible to Muslims, (3) intelligible to Christians. That I have only been partially successful means that one must keep trying, not that one must not try. For a similar point on a smaller scale, compare the reference to Montgomery Watt, below, n. 42.

inter alia, that the scholar studied religion but did not (at least, qua scholar) participate in it. Most of the significant academic advances in the study of religion before World War I or thereabouts were made by the secular rationalist. In mid-twentieth century, on the other hand, he is joined, if not superseded, by the explicit Christian as a student of non-Christian religions, or at least by the serious searcher as a student of all religions, in the West. Seventy-five years ago it was widely held in universities that a necessary qualification for an "impartial" or scientific study of religion, including the religions of other communities, was that the student be without a faith of his own, be not *engagé;* at the present time, the contrary view is not unfamiliar.[28]

Secondly, the Western scholar in this as in other fields is being joined by investigators from other civilizations—where the secular-religious dichotomy of the West does not, or does not so fully, obtain. In the Muslim world, India, the Buddhist countries, writers in this field will largely write, one may expect, as Muslims, as Hindus, or as Buddhists.[29] This much at least may be conceded, that along with the academic tradition of detached secular study of religion, there is growing in both Christendom and elsewhere a religiously related scholarship of religious diversity.[30] To some extent in the future these studies, it would seem,

[28] When it became known that a certain chair of comparative religion was held by a professor who was a Unitarian Christian, two opposite reactions could be observed by the present writer among colleagues: one, that by being a Unitarian "at least he would be less prejudiced [than a more orthodox Christian] in his work"; the other, that a man who had not seen the point of his own religion could hardly be expected to see the point of other people's.

[29] Communist scholars, e.g., from China, may write in a non-religious fashion, but not as non-*engagés.* Since I am of those that hold Confucians to be in fact, as such, religious men, non-Communist Chinese writers would seldom prove exceptions to the general principle.

[30] One recent example among many: Franz König (ed.), *Christus und die Religionen der Erde: Handbuch der Religionsgeschichte* (3 vols.; Freiburg, 1956²). A Muslim example: 'Abd Allāh Dirāz, *al-Dīn: Buḥūth Mumahhidah li-darāsat ta'rīkh al-adyān* (Cairo, 1952). More recently: Ahmad 'Abdullāh al-Masdūsī, *Maẓāhib-i 'Ālam* (Karachi, 1958). More generally, one may compare such earlier names as Max Müller, Tylor, Fraser, Durkheim, and may one not add Freud, with such recent ones as Otto, Kraemer, Wach, Van der Leeuw, Eliade, etc.? Further, one may note how little of any significance at the present time is being put forward on religion by secularists, over against the very considerable activity in nascent departments of religion and by divinity schools and the churches, especially in America. Not many decades ago it was virtually standard that the academic writer take

45

are to be carried out by religious people for religious people.

The third aspect of this development is that even the secular rationalist is coming to be seen as a person like another: not a god, not a superior impersonal intellect, monarch of all it surveys, but a man with a particular point of view. Secular rationalism may be the right road, may be the Truth as it claims to be; but it has come to be felt that there is no a priori intellectual or universal reason for supposing so from the start, so that it may sit in unchallenged judgment on equally massive and venerated traditions, Christian, Hindu, or whatever, that make the same claim. The decline of Western Europe's world position, the rise of existentialist philosophies and moods, the Western "return to religion," the rise of communism, and the resurgence of Eastern civilizations on a religious base, have all conspired to bring about this new situation, wherein the secular intellectual, like the religious believer, takes his place as a member of one group of men, one of the world's communities, looking out upon the others.

Each writer in this field is beginning to be recognized and to recognize himself as the exponent or champion of one tradition in a world of other persons expounding or championing others.[31]

---

for granted that religion is a fallacy, the problem being to explain it away in terms of something else; recent books on the matter take it as at least a mystery, if not as an accepted commitment. Studies of individual religions by clerics, such as Cragg (Islam) and De Lubac (Buddhism) cannot be matched today by secularists' works.

[31] In the case of Islamic studies, this general point may be illustrated with reference to two of the West's ablest scholars, Gibb and Von Grunebaum. That the former speaks in a situation of a "we" reporting about "they" is made explicit, with the use of these actual pronouns, in the Preface to his *Modern Trends in Islam* (Chicago, 1947), pp. x–xii. Part of Gibb's greatness as a scholar lies in his clear awareness of Islam as the faith of living persons, and his incorporating this into the Western academic tradition; he was one of the first to visit the Muslim world regularly (until World War I, he spent a sizable period every winter in Cairo, and was a member of the Egyptian Academy; this was true also of Massignon, another of the pioneers in introducing the personalist sense into Western Islamics). Gibb's "we," cited above, refers to the Christian community in the West. Von Grunebaum studies Islamic civilization as a conscious representative of the Western academic tradition ("we") confronting the Islamic tradition ("they"). He knows that the former tradition is on the defensive in the modern world; it has his loyalty and esteem, while he recognizes clearly that other traditions have other men's loyalty and esteem in a comparable, if for him less justified, fashion. His concern is essentially comparative civilization rather than comparative religion, the Western academic tradition being the crowning aspect of Western civilization and Islam the foun-

III

The next step follows rather closely. When both the writer and that about which he writes become personal, so does the relationship between them. As we have said, the present position is an encounter.[32] When persons or human communities meet, there arises a need to communicate. What had been a description is therefore in process of becoming a dialogue.

To talk about people is not the same as to talk to them; nor is this quite the same as to talk with them. The need for these last two steps in comparative religion is beginning to be felt, only gradually perhaps in universities but urgently by the churches. The word "dialogue" has actually been coming much to the fore in recent years, with both the Roman Catholic church[33] and the Protestant.[34] Major movements are afoot. It

dation aspect of Islamic civilization; our argument is not seriously affected by this point. The "we-they" theme runs through much of his writing on Islam, coming perhaps into clearest focus in a paper read to the Conference on Near East History held at the School of Oriental and African Studies, London University, 1958, not yet published.

[32] Note C. A. O. van Nieuwenhuijze, "Frictions between Presuppositions in Cross-cultural Encounters: The Case of Islamology" ("Institute of Social Studies Publications on Social Change," No. 12 [The Hague, 1958]), pp. 66–67: "We must persistently remain aware of our own presuppositions in our Islamic studies. We must consider our studies an encounter first and foremost, even rather than as an attempt at understanding, let alone interpretation." This quotation is taken from a paper commenting *inter alia* on the International Islamic Colloquium, Lahore, 1958—which I also attended. The almost fantastic developments of that conference would lend themselves rather readily to analysis in the terms being put forward in the present essay, I suggest. The conference in its discussion on Islam by Muslims and others ("non-Muslims") displayed every variety of an impersonal/ it, impersonal/they, we/they, we/you, we-all relationship pattern, and collapsed because of a failure both to clarify these and to clarify which was to obtain.

[33] There are many instances throughout the world. As a friend of mine who is a priest puts it, "The notions of dialogue and encounter are 'in the air' these days." A practical example, in relation primarily to Islam: the summer sessions (International Seminars) at Tioumliline, Morocco, since 1956. An example at the level of intellectual statement, of theory: Louis Gardet and M.-M. Anawati, *Introduction à la théologie musulmane: Essai de théologie comparée* (Paris, 1948)—Note in their announcement of purpose: "C'est un fait que le dialogue ne s'est que peu engagé encore entre la culture occidentale (chrétienne ou déchristianisée) et la culture arabo-musulmane. Tout cependant semble le requérir" (p. 6), and again in their conclusion, the word "dialogue" being taken up again in the final and perhaps culminating sentence of the book.

[34] Again there are many instances, throughout the world. The word "dialogue" (also "encounter") has become popular with the World Council of

is perhaps too early yet to say whether this is the form into which the earlier unilateral preaching of the evangelistic missionary movement is being transformed; there seem to be forces working in that direction, not the least being the vitality of the faiths addressed. Might it not be that the next step in missions would necessarily be one where one religious group says to another, "This is what we have seen of the truth, this is what God has done for us; tell us what you have seen, what God has done for you; and let us discuss it together"?[35] Provided that this is sincere, it seems entirely legitimate; though if a participant privately hoped or believed that out of a genuine discussion the other side would come to a preference for his side, then it may still be evangelical. In addition to this type of mutuality, perhaps with some ecclesiastical commitment, more and more there are independent dialogues, or encounters where the spirit is not persuasive but inquiring, where members of two faiths or groups of members meet simply to learn. The same question as before may be put, but in this case the objective is one's own enrichment, rather than the other group's, or the enrichment of all but without any transfer of allegiance. Indeed, even on an institutionalized scale, there are incipient encounters where the specified purpose is the needed but difficult matter of the groups' simply learning how they may live together in mutual respect and collaboration.[36]

Churches and International Missionary Council, Geneva, as well as in less formal or authoritative circles. In fact, so common has the terminology become in some Christian thinking that in a recent academic book it is even used as a verb: "It is good for us Christians [note the pronoun] to have these other missionary religions dispute the Gospel. . . . The present dispute brings the issues and differences among religions out in the open so that the genuine Christian has to dialogue with the genuine Jew, the true Muslim, the best Hindu and the real Buddhist . . ." (concluding paragraph of Edmund Perry, *The Gospel in Dispute: The Relation of Christian Faith to Other Missionary Religions* [New York, 1958]). The author is chairman of the Department of History and Literature of Religions, Northwestern University.

[35] Some modification in the phraseology would be needed in certain cases, e.g., that of Theravadin Buddhists; but the substance of the approach is not altered.

[36] Instances of friendly coming together are the World Congress of Faiths, established in 1936 in London by Sir Francis Younghusband and now with a considerable membership, program, and institutionalized life; at an academic level the Union for the Study of Great Religions, founded in 1950 in Oxford by Spalding, Radhakrishnan, and Raven; etc. Instances where

To situations of these kinds the comparative religionist may respond in various ways, though to me it hardly seems reasonable that he not respond at all. First, he may participate in the dialogue, as a member of one or other group. In a meeting between, let us say, Christians and Buddhists, it is clear that the conversation would proceed the better if the latter contingent included a well-qualified Buddhist student of comparative religion. One would hardly organize a dialogue with Hindus without inviting Radhakrishnan. Indeed, in a sense all members of the encounter are in effect expected *ipso facto* to end up as in some sort comparative religionists; presumably some of them might well start so. In the Christian case specifically (and to some extent the same would apply in theory to the Muslims, though in practice today it would clearly not) it would be felt by some that the comparative religionist would be out of place as a protagonist in any encounter. Such a feeling has been due to two things: the Western tradition of academic non-involvement, on which we have already commented, and the Christian tradition of exclusivism and proselytism. I would argue that these last two are not (or will become not) obligatory elements of the Christian faith, and indeed my personal view would be that the very value and even the purpose of Christian dialogue with other faiths may well be a Christian learning at last to apprehend one's own faith fully and loyally (and perhaps more truly?) and simultaneously to appreciate the quality and even the ultimate validity (in the eyes of God) of others'. Many today say that this is in principle not possible. I venture to believe that it is[37] and that dialogue may be an avenue of the church's reaching it.

Whatever one's own view, however, I do not see how either I or anyone else, on either academic or moral grounds, can possibly legislate that, let us say, Hendrik Kraemer be not allowed

---

specifically two religions are involved are the Council on Christians and Jews, founded in 1923, and the Continuing Committee on Muslim-Christian Cooperation, set up in 1954 as a result of a meeting at Bhandun, Lebanon, sponsored by the American Friends of the Middle East.

[37] First, I reject the view that a rule may be set up a priori that in qualifying as an adequate scholar of comparative religion there is involved withdrawing from one's own community; second, I hold that one has not fully understood the faith of a community other than one's own until one has seen how that faith can serve (does serve, has served) as the channel between God and those persons.

to participate in a Christian encounter with other faiths, or can possibly deny him the right to hold his chair.[38] I do not at all like his views, but I feel that I must refute them, not suppress them.[39]

In the other sort of dialogue, where the purpose is mutual understanding, amity, and collaboration, the comparative religionist may clearly participate. One would hardly argue that either a Christian or a Muslim scholar in this field would be out of place in the recently established Continuing Committee on Muslim-Christian Co-operation, or a Christian or Jewish scholar on the Council of Christians and Jews. He would do so in his private capacity, no doubt; but presumably he would both learn something, and contribute something, qua scholar.

The second role that the representative of our studies may play in the encounter between faiths is that of chairman. For this Kraemer would be disqualified by his views, but also he would not choose the post. Others of us, however, may aspire to

[38] When he wrote *The Christian Message in a Non-Christian World* (London, 1938), he was Professor of the History of Religions at the University of Leiden—a post for which one could hardly argue that he was not qualified.

[39] Perhaps, however, it is legitimate not merely to argue against his conclusions but to urge against his position from the start the general principle that an outsider cannot understand a civilization or a great religion unless he approaches it with humility and love. Such a principle does not apply, I must admit, to a phenomenon such as fascism. I personally find so axiomatic a differentiation between at least the great religions, with their long historical record behind them of human achievement, and such things as fascism that I see no practical problem here. But perhaps there is still an intellectual problem, so that the sentence in the text stands. Until that intellectual problem is resolved, my statement in note 37, above, needs some refinement on the intellectual level. I feel that adequate writing about a religion by an outsider requires an imaginative recognition that if, say, I had been born a Hindu I would presumably remain a Hindu, if born a Muslim I would presumably remain a Muslim, but if born a German I like to think that I would not have been a Nazi. Can this judgment be intellectualized and objectively justified? That it is an objective statement can be shown statistically: a large number of Germans did reject naziism. Even more important, those Germans who rejected it are all those whom one admires, whom one could take as friends; whereas those Hindus and Muslims whom I admire, who are my friends (and indeed whom Christians generally must admire, and do take as friends), remain Hindus and Muslims. (And probably it is good that they so remain.)

My statement above must not be taken to exclude the point that if I were a Hindu or a Muslim, presumably I would be a reforming one (just as in fact I am a reforming Christian). Since every religion has to do with transcendent reality, it is part of the truth of that religion to be dissatisfied with its extant forms.

qualify—and indeed to regard this qualification as almost the essence of our work. One objective of training might be formulated as equipping the student with such an understanding of at least two religions, and of the problems of relationship, that he can serve as a mediator or interpreter between them, or at least as a kind of broker helping them to interpret themselves to each other. There is need today for men so equipped, and where else are they to derive the training? Moreover, how better could one's competence in this discipline be tested?

In fact, in one or other of these roles not only might the scholar of comparative religion seem professionally involved; perhaps the department of comparative religion may become institutionally so. It is perhaps not unlikely that over the next, say, twenty-five years, departments of comparative religion in various parts of the world will formally become places where such dialogues deliberately and explicitly take place, formalizing and systematizing the intellectual encounter between representatives of diverse traditions. In North America such a process has already begun at McGill, Chicago, and Harvard. The move will be effectively launched only when there are counterparts in Asia.[40]

The third role is that of observer. If the comparative religionist chooses not to participate in or to moderate the dialogues that are in fact increasingly taking place, at least he can hardly fail to take a (professional) interest in what is going on. It is part of the contemporary history of the religions (and conceivably one of the most profound matters in the whole history of religion) that they are encountering each other, both on systematized occasion and informally in the coffee houses of the world. And even on the sidelines he may find himself being asked at least to provide the theory for those that are practically involved. People wishing to talk together across religious frontiers have been finding that their conceptions of one another's faiths, their capacity to explicate their own faiths in terms that can be understood by outsiders, and the concepts of mutual dis-

[40] On the whole, Asian religions and communities have been considerably more ready for collaboration and mutual study than has the West. It is the formal, academic pattern of these at the level of scholarship that is here in question. The Union for the Study of the Great Religions (cf. n. 36, above) has begun to be active in this matter, particularly in Pakistan and India.

course available to them jointly, are inadequate. They turn to comparative religion to supply this.

At an even more withdrawn level, the scholar is presented with the task of conceptualizing the dynamic processes at work, and of discerning and again conceptualizing whatever new may emerge.

In this human situation is elucidated my earlier contention that a statement about a religion, in order to be valid, must be intelligible and acceptable to those within. In order to be sincere, and of any use, it must also of course be intelligible and acceptable to the outsider who makes it. When Muslims and Buddhists meet, what is needed are a statement of Islam that Muslims can recognize as valid and Buddhists can recognize as meaningful, and similarly a statement about Buddhism that Buddhists can acknowledge and Muslims understand. In any dialogue the participants, the chairman, and the writer of books that all of these will read must move towards this if intercommunication is to proceed.

This can be generalized so that herein is posed one of the fundamental tasks of our studies today. I would formulate it thus: *it is the business of comparative religion to construct statements about religion that are intelligible within at least two traditions simultaneously.*[41] This is not easy, it has not been done systematically in the past and almost not done at all; but it is intellectually important and historically urgent.

[41] The following extracts from the regulations for the degree of Ph.D. in Islamic-Studies at McGill University illustrate one attempt to formalize this kind of consideration. In this case only one religion is in question, and attention is given to the relationship between the Islamic tradition and the Western academic tradition. Speaking of what the Institute of Islamic Studies here regards as the inadequacy of a doctorate's only applying the form of the latter to the substance of the former, the memorandum goes on to say: "Its ambition would be to encompass something of the substance of both Western and Islamic traditions, and also something of the form of both. . . . In the matter of form he [the candidate] should not only satisfy the principle of a Western doctorate, but also produce work that would maintain continuity with the Islamic tradition. It is the task . . . of the Institute to strive for the construction of new forms that will subsume but transcend the present pattern on both sides: new forms, that is, that will neither betray the Western academic tradition nor distort the Islamic. The product of research must be relevant to both, significant to both, and cogent in both. . . . [The] thesis should be recognizable in both traditions as a constructive advance." For the doctorate in comparative religion, formal regulations have not yet been adopted for this point, but the same principles

Since the scholar presumably works from a university, that is, within the academic tradition, the statement that he produces must first of all be meaningful and cogent within that tradition. That is, it must satisfy his own trained and inquiring mind, and must satisfy all the most rigorous standards of scholarship. In the particular case where the encounter is between the academic tradition of the West and a particular religion, the statement that is evolved must satisfy each of two traditions independently and transcend them both by satisfying both simultaneously. In the case of an encounter between two religious groups, let us say for example Christianity and Islam, the scholar's creativity must rise to the point where his work is cogent within three traditions simultaneously: the academic, the Christian, and the Muslim. This is not easy, but I am persuaded that both in principle and in practice it can be done.[42]

---

would obtain, with the added complication that the candidate must satisfy three traditions: that of Western scholarship and also those of at least two religions. In the case of living religions, an acceptable doctoral thesis would, among other requirements, have to satisfy examiners representing each of the traditions concerned.

[42] There is an example of a successful attempt, on a small scale—in fact, on simply one particular point, though an important one: W. Montgomery Watt, in the Introduction to his *Muḥammad at Mecca* (Oxford, 1953), p. x, writes, "I have refrained from using the expressions 'God says' and 'Muhammad says' when referring to the Qur'ān, and have simply said 'the Qur'ān says.'" The device may seem minor and almost too simple, but I would urge its significance. To anyone familiar with the history of Western biographies of the Prophet, with its long tale of vituperation and certainly of totally reckless distance from the attitudes of Muslims as a community of persons, it is particularly striking to have a scholar write explicitly in the awareness that he is writing also for a Muslim audience, and take pains to write in a way that they can accept. "This book will be considered by at least three classes of readers: those who are concerned with the subject as historians, and those who approach it primarily as Muslims or Christians" (*ibid.*; this is the opening sentence of the book). The paragraph from which these two sentences are taken indicates, however, that the author is picturing his situation to himself as one of avoiding the issue between Christians and Muslims rather than (so far as wording goes) solving it. He does not seem to realize that the form of his presentation has transcended the separate viewpoints, not merely evaded two of them ("In order to avoid deciding whether the Qur'ān is or is not the Word of God, I have refrained . . ."). Is this perhaps the first time that a Western or Christian scholar was consciously and deliberately writing in such a way as to be read by these three groups?

For the same attempt on a larger scale, compare my work mentioned in note 27, above, in which every sentence in the book was thought out so as to be, if possible, cogent in all three traditions.

This kind of constructive thinking is necessary in order to provide the intellectual basis for the meetings between communities that are today taking place. Like other intellectual advance instigated by actual problems of evolving human conditions, however, it has worth in itself, and implications far outreaching the immediate issues. In principle, the drive is toward the construction of an intellectual statement (or history) of the diverse religions of mankind that ideally does justice to all of them as well as standing independently, a statement that will be cogent to a reasonable man who is a member of any faith or of none. This leads us on to our fourth major consideration, where the personalization of our studies with which we began eventuates in their attaining fully human status, overcoming the local or particularist. In this lies the culmination of this development of our work, and to it we now turn.

IV

The emergence of dialogue is important not only in itself but for its further implications. Once it is achieved, its significance transcends the achievement, opening the way to a still newer stage. For a dialogue may lead (in some individual cases has led already) to reconciliation, to an enlarged sense of community. In any case, and at the least, it implies articulateness on two sides. This is incipient, and major. No longer is the prosecution of these studies exclusively a western prerogative. Japanese are studying Eskimo animism and Christianity, Muslims are diagnosing Western secularism, the theorizing of Hindus about comparative religion is becoming widely known. Muslims, Hindus, and Buddhists are learning to talk to Christian and Western scholars, as well as being talked to; and in the process are studying religious diversity itself. Thus the Western scholar is slowly coming to have not only an Asian (or African) informant as his source, an Asian critic as his audience, an Asian scholar as his teacher, but, perhaps most significantly of all, an Asian colleague as his collaborator.

Certainly we are only at its beginning, but the long-term trend promises to be towards a transformed situation, where an international body of scholars writes for a world audience. This essentially new and potentially highly significant emergence brings to light what I see as the culmination of the contemporary transformation. As with the other stages, it makes vivid what was always in principle true but hardly grasped.

I have argued that one cannot study religion from above, only from alongside or from within—only as a member of some group. Today the group of which the student recognizes himself as a member is capable of becoming, even is in process of becoming, world-wide—and interfaith. This is the significant matter.

For once the community becomes large enough, and if consciousness keeps pace, that process is fulfilled whereby the study is no longer an objective inquiry carried on from the outside, but a human study carried on from within. Even a face-to-face dialogue gives way to a side-by-side conversation, where scholars of different faiths no longer confront each other but collaborate in jointly confronting the universe, and consider together the problems in which all of them are involved.

For finally it will be recognized that in comparative religion man is studying himself. The fact of religious diversity is a human problem, common to us all. It is becoming an incorporated, internal part of the fact of being a Christian that other intelligent, devout, and righteous men are Muslims, Hindus, Buddhists. Even the non-religious man is engaged in living in a world where his fellows are of unreconciled faiths. Every man is personally involved in all man's diversity. Man here is studying one of the most profound, one of the most perplexing, one of the potentially most explosive aspects of his own modern situation. We all are studying the fact that our human community is divided within itself religiously.

The practitioner of comparative religion, then, I am suggesting, may become no longer an observer vis-à-vis the history of the diverse religions of distant or even close communities, but rather a participant—in the multiform religious history of the only community there is, humanity. *Comparative religion may become the disciplined self-consciousness of man's variegated and developing religious life.*

We may look now for a history not so much of the disparate religions but of man's religiousness. Such a history should be persuasive to students of that total history, themselves from diverse faiths. It should be such and they should be such that they can recognize and acknowledge their own separate communities within it, and at the same time recognize and acknowledge the totality, of which also they are learning to be part. Such a history should in particular trace and clarify—even explain— the rise, at a certain period of human history, of the great religions as separate entities. Perhaps also sheerly by being written it would give some intellectualization to the fact that again, in the present period of human history, those great religions seem in some degree to be in process of ceasing to be quite so separate, even perhaps of ceasing to be quite so surely entities.[43]

The student of comparative religion begins with the postulate that it is possible to understand a religion other than one's own.[44] In our day, this postulate is being tested—urgently, severely, by our concrete human situation. We are called upon to make good our claim, in practice, and quickly. To meet this challenge demands that we rethink our purposes, recast our basic concepts. But there is also the promise that if we do meet it, the results may contribute to that largest of contemporary problems, the turning of our nascent world society into a world community.

A religious history of man has yet to be written, concerning itself with the development of us all rather than primarily with the development of each. It is interesting to note, however, that titles are beginning to be phrased as "the religions of *man*" and the like.[45] And in other ways the work of individual scholars has begun to move in this direction.[46]

[43] That each of the religions of the world is in some sense a distinct entity is a commonly accepted notion. On examination it proves that this idea has come into historical acceptance gradually, and there is perhaps some reason to speculate as to whether it will persist in its current form. I have examined the question at some length in the lectures referred to above (n. 24).

[44] If this postulate be false, then the whole study must of course be called off. Admittedly, one would be left with what we began this essay with, the factual data of the *Encyclopaedia*, but with the added proclamation now that one does not and cannot understand what the data signify. This would constitute a formidable and no doubt growing discipline of the history of the externalia of religion, and there could be a comparative religious externalia. The work of the current school of phenomenologists in Europe would continue to have significance.

[45] Two examples: John B. Noss, *Man's Religions* (New York, 1949, and subsequent editions); Huston Smith, *The Religions of Man* (New York, 1958), cf. n. 15, above. Compare also Paul Hutchinson's essay "How Mankind Worships" referred to in n. 16, above.

[46] Younger scholars, perhaps particularly in North America, seem to be taking up a relationship to their work of some such kind. For example, Philip H. Ashby, *The Conflict of Religions* (New York, 1955), the first work of the first scholar in this field at Princeton, is a discussion "concerning the

Presently may there be a symposium in which scholars from different faiths will write chapters not each on his own faith but perhaps each on other aspects of the total development, in a way agreeable to all?[47]

It would, of course, be an oversimplification to hold that an over-all development such as has been here outlined has gone forward quite straightforwardly and steadily. I do suggest, however, that it is in fact possible to characterize any study of a religion other than one's own, or of interrelationships, as falling under one or other of these headings. I suggest also that there has been on the whole a gradual movement in the direction indicated. I contend further that clarity here will prove of major benefit. We must become conscious, and self-conscious, on this matter. Students would do well to ask themselves, concerning any account or any project that they meet, in which category it falls: impersonal/it, impersonal/they, we/they, we/you, we-both, or we-all. A writer should clarify in his own mind which kind of book or article he is proposing to write; and an organizer, which kind of university department, of conference, of journal, he is proposing to run.

Though the various principles that we have adumbrated are beginning to be recognized, the performance, one must confess, is as yet sadly inadequate. It will be a good while yet before anything is achieved on the level of interreligious communication and dialogue, let alone on that of multireligious consciousness,

---

possible contributions of the religions of the world to the amelioration of the problems of mankind" (p. 192; opening sentence of the concluding chapter); the author is concerned to show that man (*sic*) can meet the terrible problems that confront him today if he can replace the "conflict" among his various religions with a "combined witness" (p. viii). The book is implicitly written for believing members of the four largest communities (Christian, Muslim, Hindu, Buddhist) equally—this is something new.

[47] The first step towards this might be a collaborative work on two faiths; let us say Christianity and Islam, written jointly by a Christian and a Muslim. If it is possible, as I have argued, for a Christian student to write something on Islam that Muslims can acknowledge, and therefore possible also in principle (although it has not yet been done) for a Muslim to do the same on Christianity, then presumably a joint study of the two faiths and of the relationships between them could be produced by a Christian and a Muslim working in collaboration. This should be quite striking. Presumably this is the kind of work that would lay the intellectual foundation for bringing into being the human partnership at which a movement such as the Continuing Committee on Muslim-Christian Co-operation is aiming.

that can be compared for quality to the impressive monologue of the *Encyclopaedia*. When a work does appear worthy of typifying achievement in this realm, we predict that it will be written by a person who has seen and felt, and is morally, spiritually, and intellectually capable of giving expression to, the fact that we—all of us—live together in a world in which not they, not you, but *some of us* are Muslims, some are Hindus, some are Jews, some are Christians. If he is really great, he will perhaps be able to add, some of us are Communists, some inquirers.

If the great religions are true, or even if any one of them is, then such a work is possible; and if it is written, it will be essentially true. For have we not been told that men are brothers, that in the eyes of God[48] the human community is the only real community there is? And that the two matters of supreme importance are the relations among persons within that total community, and the relations between men and God?

[48] One might equally say, in the eye of reason. In line with this, one might then add to the preceding sentence, "or if the rationalist tradition is true."

The Supreme Being:
Phenomenological Structure
and Historical Development

When one speaks in a historical-religious way of the Supreme Being of the so-called primitive peoples, one usually means by this the Celestial Supreme Being.

The sky, in its unbounded immensity, in its perennial presence, in its wondrous luminosity, is particularly well suited to suggest to the mind of man the idea of sublimity, of incomparable majesty, of a sovereign and mysterious power. The sky elicits in man the feeling of a theophany. This is the feeling of a manifestation of the divine, which finds adequate expression in the notion of a Supreme Being.

On the other hand, the notion of a Supreme Being is not exhausted in the image of the Celestial Being. In the following pages I propose to show that there exist various distinct forms of the Supreme Being and that the Celestial Being is just one of them.

Forty years ago, when I began to study the notion of a Supreme Being, I insisted especially on its uranic aspects.[1] The Supreme Being was for me essentially a mythical personification of the sky. The evolution of my thought in this matter has

---

[1] I refer especially to my book entitled *L'Essere celeste nelle credenze dei popoli primitivi* (Rome, 1922).

come about without any modification of the original theoretical basis of my position. For example, while I am now in partial agreement with Fr. Wilhelm Schmidt as to the non-reducibility of the Supreme Being to the Celestial Being, it must be noticed that the convergence of positions is extrinsic to them and limited to the specific point.[2] Aside from the question of *Urmonotheismus*, which I have considered again recently,[3] with respect to the notion of the Supreme Being I am still of the opinion that it is not mainly the product of logico-causal thought, as Schmidt held, but rather that this notion is the product of mythical thought. I am still opposed to the theory that the notion of the Supreme Being arises out of man's supposed intellectualistic need of becoming aware of the origin and wherefore of things. In what follows it will be clarified that the notion of a Supreme Being springs from man's existential needs.

The above argument is also valid with respect to other investigators, who starting from different theoretical premises have also recognized the non-reducibility of the Supreme Being to the Celestial Being. Gerardus van der Leeuw held a similar position from the point of view of religious phenomenology. Van der Leeuw delineated the phenomenological structure of the Supreme Being and distinguished it from the structure of Yahweh.[4] The specific structure of the Supreme Being is especially represented, for Van der Leeuw, by the various Supreme Beings that one can find among peoples of inferior civilization. This structure, however, is not limited to them but rather extends beyond the primitive world and also comprehends, for example, the Supreme Being as defined by Robespierre at the time of the French Revolution in opposition to the cult of Divine Reason. The structure of Yahweh is, for Van der Leeuw, totally different. The Supreme Being is a distant god, removed in space and time, a static immanence rather than an active presence. Yahweh, on the other hand, is not only a power but also a will, not only a person but also a personality, a live personality, a

[2] Father Wilhelm Schmidt, *Handbuch der vergleichenden Religionswissenschaft* (Münster i.W., 1930), pp. 202 ff.

[3] Raffaele Pettazzoni, "Das Ende des Urmonotheismus?" *Numen*, III, (1956), 156.

[4] Gerardus van der Leeuw, "Die Struktur der Vorstellung des sogenannten höchsten Wesens," *Archiv für Religionswissenschaft*, XXIX (1931), 79–107.

live god operating on and ever present to man, a hostile and jealous god, not without something of the demonic.

This characterization of Yahweh abstracts completely from his uranic aspect, and also from every other naturalistic aspect of the personality of the Supreme Being. The distance between the two structures leaves us perplexed, however, and we ask ourselves if the separation between the two structures is so neat. Creativity is postulated as a specific character of the Supreme Being. But Yahweh also is a creator; Yahweh's very creation *ex nihilo* is found comparable to the creation of some Supreme Beings of primitive peoples who create by means of pure thought and will.[5] On the other hand, a salient trait of the personality of Yahweh is the severe surveillance he maintains on all human actions, on all human words, on all human thoughts, scrutinizing "hearts and kidneys" inexorably. Moreover, this all-seeing and omniscience as applied to human conduct issues into divine sanctions. But in its turn, this last character of Yahweh is likewise one of the more constant attributes of the Supreme Beings of primitive peoples.[6] Robespierre's address to the Commune of Paris at the convention of 1793 evidences that his Supreme Being also had this same character: "L'homme pervers se croit sans cesse environné d'un témoin puissant et terrible auquel il ne peut échapper, qui le voit et le veille, tandis que les hommes sont livrés au sommeil. ..."[7] How can one isolate this "structure" and separate it from its biblical antecedents, when—to cite only one of the many passages—one can read in the book of Isaiah (29:15): "Woe to those who hide deep from the Lord their counsel, whose deeds are in the dark, and who say, 'Who sees us? Who knows us?' "

It is in this character of irascibility and of vindictiveness, which not even the prophets can completely transfigure into their ideal of a God of justice, that Yahweh has been compared to the Vedic Varuna.[8] On the other hand, for Van der Leeuw,

[5] Cf. Raffaele Pettazzoni, "L'Idée de création et la notion d'un Être créateur chez les Californiens," *Proceedings of the Thirty-second International Congress of Americanists*, 1956 (Copenhagen, 1958).

[6] Raffaele Pettazzoni, *The All-knowing God* (London, 1956), *passim*.

[7] F. A. Aulard, *Le Culte de la raison et le culte de l'Être Suprème* (Paris, 1892), pp. 285 f.

[8] A. Titius, "Die Anfänge der Religion bei Ariern und Israeliten," *Studien zur systematischen Theologie*, XVI (Heidelberg, 1934), 34.

Varuna is the maximum approximation of Indian religious thought to the structure of the Supreme Being.[9] It appears, then, that the alleged difference in structure between Yahweh and the Supreme Being is rather a fluid one and that in this matter it is very easy to be misled by purely hypothetical and genial but non-objective suggestions.

Because of his demonic character, Yahweh can also be compared to other gods and Supreme Beings of inferior civilizations. For example, the Aztec god Tezcatlipoca, a despotic numen, vengeful, implacable, violent in his chastisement, pleased by suffering, has seemed to the ethnologist H. Dietschy "ein alttestamentlicher Gott."[10] Chungichnish (or Chinigchinish), a god of the Luiseño (Southern California) already known to the Franciscan missionaries, has been considered by A. L. Kroeber as "a living god that watches and punishes, a kind of Jahve."[11] The same character has been noted in the Supreme Being of the Cuna Indians of Darien (Panama). This god, named Diolele, is a severe punisher of sins; omniscient, there is no sin that escapes his sanction or sinner who can find compassion in him. Erland Nordenskiöld has written that this conception of a god so inexorably severe seems to be more akin to the austere spirit of the Calvinistic creed than that of the more tolerant Catholicism.[12] It is true that these comparisons of similarity are anthropologically rather than phenomenologically derived. But, this even points to the danger that phenomenological structures may become as superficially empty and purely formal as are anthropological comparisons. It is not without reason that Van der Leeuw, the great master of religious phenomenology, prescribed that religious phenomenology should constantly appeal to history. Phenomenology, he wrote, is interpretation; but phenomenological hermeneutics "becomes pure art and fantasy,

[9] Van der Leeuw, *op. cit.*, p. 97.

[10] H. Dietschy, "Mensch und Gott bei mexikanischen Indianern," *Anthropos*, XXXV/XXXVI (1940/41), 336.

[11] A. L. Kroeber, *Handbook of the Indians of California* (Bureau of American Ethnology, Smithsonian Institution, Bull. 78 [Washington, 1925]), p. 656. G. Boscana, "Chinigchinich," in A. Robinson, *Life in California* (New York, 1846).

[12] Erland Nordenskiöld, *Picture-Writings and Other Documents of the Cuna Indians* ("Comparative Ethnological Studies," Vol. VII, No. 2 [Göteborg, 1930]), pp. 8, 13.

as soon as it is separated from the control of philological-archeological hermeneutics."[13] In the spirit of the constant process of auto-revision recommended by Van der Leeuw the phenomenology of the Supreme Being likewise needs to be revised and modified in accordance with the progress of the historical disciplines, in this case especially of ethnology conceived as non-philological history, as the history of non-literate peoples.

The structural dualism introduced by Van der Leeuw in the phenomenology of the Supreme Being is particularly evident in the contrast between the *otiositas* which is attributed to many Supreme Beings of the ethnological world, and the intense activity of Yahweh. He is always vigilant, always ready to intervene in human affairs. But this interventionism, this perennial surveillance, the speedy sanctions with the presupposition of omniscience is likewise a common character of many ethnological Supreme Beings.[14] On the other hand, the laziness of several Supreme Beings is a secondary condition that follows an initial phase of extraordinary activity such as the creation of the world.

The phenomenology of the Supreme Being is not exhausted by the alternatives of a Supreme Being who is creator of the world (and eventually a candidate to successive inactivity) and a Supreme Being who is omnipresent and omniscient with the explicit vocation to interventionism. If Yahweh, creator of the world and punisher of human transgressions, unites both structures it is because we are really dealing not with different structures, but with two aspects of a unique two-sided structure, one cosmic and the other human: on the one side the creation of the world and its conservation *in statu quo*, as a condition that guarantees the existence and endurance of the universe; on the other side the establishment of the social order and its restora-

[13] Gerardus van der Leeuw, *Phänomenologie der Religion* (Tübingen, 1933), p. 642: "Soll die Phänomenologie ihre Aufgabe vollbringen, so hat sie die immerwährende *Korrektur* der gewissenschaftesten philologischen, archäologischen Forschung sehr nötig. Sie muss stets bereit sein, sich der Konfrontation mit dem Tatsachenmaterial zu stellen. . . . [Die] rein philologische Hermeneutik hat weniger weite Ziele als die rein phänomenologische. . . .Das phänomenologische Verständnis wird aber zur reinen Kunst oder zur leeren Phantastik, sobald [es] sich der Kontrolle durch die philologisch-archäologische Deutung entzieht" (quoting Joachim Wach, *Religionswissenschaft* [Leipzig, 1924], p. 117).

[14] Pettazzoni, *The All-knowing God, passim.*

tion when man has subverted it.[15] This subversion, with its transgressions of tribal law, with its violations of traditional norms, is a return to primitive barbarism, just as lightning, hurricanes, and other cataclysms sent as divine punishment are a suspension of cosmic order and a relapse into primordial chaos.

All of the above phenomenology is oriented toward the heavens. Yahweh, creator of the world, punisher with the flood, pacifier with the rainbow, is a Supreme Being equal to Zeus, who is a god of lightning but not the creator of the world. Many Supreme Beings are Celestial Beings, some even have names that signify the sky, as, for example, the Chinese Tien, the Mongolian Tangri, the Greek Zeus, the Roman Jupiter, and others. For these cases, my thesis that we are dealing with mythical personifications of the sky is valid, in my opinion. But, as I have already indicated, this thesis is not valid for all Supreme Beings. Not all Supreme Beings are Celestial Beings. The notion of the Supreme Being is not exhausted in the notion of a Celestial Being. For many peoples the Supreme Being is not the heavenly Father, but the Mother Earth. The Earth as universal mother and creatrix par excellence is not omniscient, that is to say that she does not have that omniscience which is rooted in all-seeing (the Greek *oida*, "I know," properly means "I have seen"). The visual omniscience which is naturally proper to the Celestial Being is proper to him because of the luminosity of the heavens. On the contrary, the earth is opaque, dark, and tenebrous. The creativity of the earth also is different from the creativity of the Celestial Being.

There is a phenomenology of the Supreme Being oriented toward the sky and there is a phenomenology of the Supreme Being oriented toward the earth. This polarity is phenomenologically legitimate because both sky and earth are theophanies, i.e., manifestations of the divine. Furthermore, this polarity is methodologically well founded because it realizes the historical premises of phenomenology (in this case the history of preliterate peoples) according to the principle that without history phenomenology tends to vanish in a more or less arbitrary subjectivism.

Behind the Heavenly Father there is a long tradition of pas-

[15] Cf. Raffaele Pettazzoni, "Myths of Beginnings and Creation Myths," *Essays on the History of Religions* (Leiden, 1954), pp. 24–36.

toral patriarchal civilization. Behind the Mother Earth there is a long tradition of agricultural matriarchal civilization. The Heavenly Father is the Supreme Being typical of the nomads who live on the products of their herds; the herds live on the pastures, and these in their turn depend on rain from the sky. The Mother Earth is the Supreme Being typical of farmers who live on the products of the soil. In more remote times prior to agriculture and to the breeding of livestock, the Supreme Being was the Lord of animals. On this Lord depended the success of the hunt. There are always in play in the notion of the Supreme Being reasons that are vital to human existence. The notion of the Supreme Being does not proceed so much from intellectualistic requirements as from existential anxieties.

These considerations are central to religious phenomenology. Phenomenology can ignore the historical-cultural sequences of ethnology, and the general theories of the development of religious history. This development can be thought of in the evolutionary (i.e., E. B. Tylor) or involutionary (i.e., W. Schmidt) sense; in either case phenomenology can ignore these theories. Van der Leeuw has written that: "Von einer historischen 'Entwicklung' der Religion, weisst die Phänomenologie nichts."[16]

On the other hand, phenomenology cannot disregard the elementary forms of civilization because the historical-cultural reality, even in the mere economic aspect, fully invades the religious life. Mircea Eliade has written that "L'agriculture est avant tout un rituel. ... Le laboureur pénètre et s'intègre dans une zone riche et sacré. Ses gestes, son travail sont responsables de graves conséquences."[17] The hunt is likewise a sacred operation in which "... l'homme doit se trouver dans un état de grâce; [elle est] l'aboutissement de longs préparatifs, où les préoccupations religieuses et magiques tiennent une place prépondérante."[18] The life of the shepherd is no less rich in religious experiences, being occasioned by the manifold risks and adventures of a wandering life. This historicism is of value for re-

[16] Van der Leeuw, *Phänomenologie der Religion*, p. 652 (quoting Wach, *op. cit.*, p. 82).

[17] Mircea Eliade, *Traité d'histoire des religions* (Paris, 1949), p. 285.

[18] Eveline Lot-Falk, *Les Rites de chasse chez les peuples sibériens* (Paris, 1953), p. 8; Fr. G. Speck, "Jagd ist eine heilige Beschäftigung," in Naskapi, *The Savage Hunters of Labrador* (Norman, Okla., 1935), cited by W. Müller, *Die Religionen der waldindianer Nordamerikas* (Berlin, 1956), p. 79.

ligious phenomenology. Existential anxiety is the common root in the structure of the Supreme Being, but this structure is historically expressed in different forms: the Lord of animals, the Mother Earth, the Heavenly Father. All these structures have profound relations with different cultural realities which have conditioned them and of which the various Supreme Beings are expressions.

The sky is extended equally over all the peoples of the world, but the sacral experience of sky is profoundly different where the sky is conceived as a cosmic complement of earth or eventually generated by the Earth (Ouranos in Hesiod), from where the heavens are felt as a diffuse, immanent presence that intrudes on man in every place and in every instant, without escape or refuge from the all-seeing eye. The earth is always and everywhere the theater of human life; but the sacral experience of earth is different where the earth tilled by man is the Mother, the nurturer, the giver of fruits and flowers for man's sustenance and joy; from the experience of the earth where it is sterile, the boundless extension of steppe whose fascination has inspired in modern times the narratives of Chekhov (*The Steppe*), the music of Borodin, and indirectly the poetry of Leopardi (*Canto notturno di un pastore errante dell'Asia*).

Phenomenology and history complement each other. Phenomenology cannot do without ethnology, philology, and other historical disciplines. Phenomenology, on the other hand, gives the historical disciplines that sense of the religious which they are not able to capture. So conceived, religious phenomenology is the religious understanding (*Verständniss*) of history; it is history in its religious dimension. Religious phenomenology and history are not two sciences but are two complementary aspects of the integral science of religion, and the science of religion as such has a well-defined character given to it by its unique and proper subject matter.[19]

[19] Cf. Pettazzoni, *Numen*, I (1954), 5.

JEAN DANIÉLOU

Phenomenology of Religions and Philosophy of Religion

The problem of a systematization of the data furnished by the history of religions has today entered a decisive phase. The immense amount of material accumulated has shown that analogous structures have been found over and over again in different religions and that it has therefore been possible to state some general laws which permit us to think in terms of an ordered unity and at the same time to differentiate the religious datum at various levels in its historical totality. Various attempts of this kind have been made, among which those of Van der Leeuw and Eliade are well known. Joachim Wach proposed a classification of types of religious experience for which there is very great interest.

Recently Henry Duméry has made an attempt to go still further.[1] Taking his position with regard to the authors we have just cited, he writes in his *Critique and Religion:*

Joachim Wach, with all that he claims for his typology, has to contend with a normative method. His manner of classification of the great forms of religious experience amounts, in fact, to a strongly rational selection. But it hardly rests on well worked out philosophical criteria. One can say as much of Van der Leeuw and Eliade, whose works are otherwise extremely valuable [*CR*, p. 204].

[1] *Critique et Religion* (Paris: Société d'Éditions d'Enseignement, 1957); *Philosophie de la Religion* (2 vols.; Paris: Presses Universitaires, 1957); *Le Problème de Dieu* (Bruges: Desclée, De Brouwer, 1957).

67

We would like to see whether Duméry has succeeded in his proposal to bring to the phenomenology of religions the philosophical justification which it lacked.

Professor Duméry's point of departure is incontestable. The history of religions today confronts us with an immense amount of material dealing with myths, symbols, and rites. All these elements have a truth value. But they must be examined critically. This allows us to discover their meaning, to verify their interrelationships, and at the same time to affirm their foundation. The philosophy of religion is in no way a substitute for religion itself. Religion is still the essential thing. Yet philosophy does bring a kind of verification to the spontaneous and existential movement of religion. It bears witness to the fact that religion is not an illusion or an emotional allurement, but that it answers to the most rigorous test of reason. It also purifies religion of its distortions.

Reason must in turn be criticized, however. Indeed, in its effort to reduce and to unify, it risks conceiving God as nothing more than the universal principle of intelligibility. And precisely this God of reason could never be the true God. Actually, as Duméry so often reiterates, the true God can never be treated as an object of reason. He is sovereign subjectivity. He is also beyond all that the mind conceives him to be. He transcends all determinations by which the mind aspires toward him.

A fruitful study might begin with these two remarks. It would consist of a dialectic in which immediate religious data would constantly be the object of critical reflection, but also in which critical reflection would constantly be referred to specific religious situations. The problem would be analogous to that of the relationships between the Bible and theology. The Bible should be continuously elaborated by theological reflection, but religious reflection must always remain in touch with the realities of the biblical witness, the first, irreducible principles upon which this reflection takes place. Austen Farrer in *The Glass of the Vision* has well demonstrated the necessity for this dual approach.

But this is precisely what appears inadequate to Henry Duméry, whose method aims at a much more radical reduction. For him, symbols and concepts do not represent two parallel lines of approach which ought to criticize each other, one arising from existence and the other from reason, but they are two stages of a hierarchy whose levels express successive modes through which the mind seeks to grasp the transcendent One. The object of criticism or of the philosophy of religion is simply to reduce these modes to the creative activity of the mind, of which they are the determining conditions, to order them in an ascending hierarchy, and thus afford them their rational justification.

Professor Duméry's criticism would then tend to be based upon the explaining of religion under its different modalities. This basis would consist in showing in these modalities the expression of the very life of the mind in its orientation toward the One, which is, for Duméry, the true name of God. Indeed, insofar as they are determinations, these modalities do not come from God. He is beyond all determination. They come, then, from the activity of the mind. They are not imposed upon it from without. It is the mind that creates them, in the order of knowledge as well as in the order of existence. But at the same time the mind must also determine itself. It cannot aspire to the inaccessible One except through a certain multiplicity. But it can manage this multiplicity all the better when it has its only source in the mind itself.

Here we come to the essential point of what we are compelled to call Henry Duméry's religious philosophy, for it is no longer just a question of a critique of religious representations but of a certain interpretation of the relationship between God and the mind. This essential point is that, for the author, not only is the mind transcendent with regard to all determining conditions, which we willingly accept, but that it is the creator of these conditions. In other words, determination, which of course is foreign to God in himself, is equally foreign to God in man and in the world, that is to say, it has its sole origin in the very mind or spirit of man. This is the principal thesis of Professor Duméry's philosophy. He repeatedly returns to his refusal to apply to God the quality of creator. Insofar as the word creator means the source of determination, it corresponds to the level of the intelligible, not of the divine, of the one-multiple, not of the one.

We can clearly see the concern which this position reflects. It entails an avoidance, in the representation of the relationships of God and the mind, of all forms of dependence which might be suggested by the world of physical causality. And this concern is quite legitimate. The relationships of God and the mind are those of two inward natures. God is sovereign inwardness. And it is in progressively interiorizing himself that man tends toward God. To be sure, his is a derived inwardness. It is the hidden presence in him of the One who is the very source of his perpetual interiorization, the attraction of the sovereign inwardness. But it is also clear that this process of interiorization expresses itself with increasing spontaneity and autonomy.

Let us apply this to the problem of determinations. It is essential to the true nature of the relations between God and man that man does not receive determinations from God, but that he provides them for himself. So the relationship remains that of two autonomous subjects. Besides, it is clear that if determination as such comes only from the intelligible, the intelligible draws from God the energy by which it is itself determined. And it also follows that through the determinations the intelligible seeks to grasp the inaccessible core of the One, in relation to which they alone take their meaning. Thus religious structures at different levels are the creations of the human mind, creations by which it aspires to the inaccessible One.

Such is the final reduction which Professor Duméry proposes to give to the science of religions a really philosophical and rational status. It does not lack positive elements. We have pointed them out in passing. One will note how the concern to defend transcendence is accompanied by that which seeks to justify rational demands. The necessity of criticizing religious representations and of pointing out their deficiency in relation to the aspired object is admirably underlined. The transcendence of freedom with regard to all objectivity which would impose itself from without responds to the claims of the best of Christian existentialism.

But there remains one fundamental difficulty which concerns the principal thesis of Duméry's system. This thesis holds that the source of determination is not in God but in the mind, for otherwise the transcendence of God could not be preserved. The consequence of this would be that there is movement of man towards God, but not of God towards man. For Duméry, God moves by the desire to bring the world into being, but does not intervene in it. There is no analogy in the order of knowledge, nor creation in the order of efficiency. It follows that religious structures are exclusively the creation of the mind, strivings by which it aims at the One through necessarily multiple representations.

One may wonder whether this takes into account the religious attitude in its essence—for the present I put aside the Christian event, which poses still other problems—for the religious attitude appears fundamentally as the expression of a dependence, whatever the point of departure for this dependence may be. Moreover, this clearly implies that the mind finds itself in conflict with some determinations which do not arise out of its own activity. Duméry has clearly foreseen this objection (*PR*, I, 30–34). He replies to it by saying that in order for the freedom of the mind not to be pure, arbitrary contingency, as it is according to Sartre, it is enough that the mind be animated by a basic dynamism toward the One: the determinations of its thought as of its action would then not have to be supplied from without. They will be the expression that the mind will give to itself with the guidance of its intelligence and its will, and they will find their norm in this orientation toward the One. This is the definition of the mind as both act and law (*PD*, pp. 100–102).

But this does not seem to do justice to the true character of the religious fact, which is to make us feel the resistance of an Other through the awareness of the laws of our own being. Sin, in the religious sense, is not a defect in the harmony of a spiritual order; it is an offense against the most holy will of God. And this implies that determinations of action and of knowledge, the good as well as the true, are not founded on the exigencies of the life of the mind, but that they express the exigencies of God. In other words, it is not in my mind that I find the ultimate basis of religious expressions. They manifest not only the vitality which turns me toward God, but first of all that which brings God to my awareness.

Now does this not seem to compromise the transcendence of God, in reducing him to determinations, and the transcendence of man in subjecting him to objective norms? Thus it would be if we accept transcendence as Duméry conceives it, but this view seems very materialistic and objectivistic. Indeed for him, transcendence is the unity which is sought through all multiplicity and for which all multiplicity is only a degradation. Yet one may ask if this transcendence, which appears at the beginning of a homogeneous series, is a true transcendence. It can, in fact, be made to agree perfectly with a rationalism or pantheism. This transcendence is that of Plotinus and of Spinoza, but in truth it is only a limit and not properly speaking a "beyond." It does not mark off that chasm between God and all else which is unbridgeable in the sense of going from man to God and bridgeable only in the sense of going from God to man—that chasm which expresses the idea of creation.

True transcendence is to be sought in another vein, that is to say, in terms of a soverign subjectivity which is both infinitely more accessible and much more susceptible to free communication without becoming diminished. It would seem that Duméry's God has to be remote in order to safeguard a transcendence which would prevent his intervention in the world. But if we are dealing with the transcendence of a sovereign subject, with a personal life, it is not immediately evident how its transcendence would be diminished by the fact that it freely communicates itself. For it remains inaccessible to all pretention of taking hold of it. Thus the transcendence of God is not altered by the creation, through which he places before him, both in its consistency and its dependence, the spiritual or psychic creation, in the manner of making it the protagonist of a dialogue and rendering it capable of an exchange of love. But this, which is the very essence of authentic transcendence, is more or less suspect for Professor Duméry, who rejects the God of dialogue (*PD*, p. 110) and the notion of creation applied to God.

The same problem arises concerning the transcendence of the mind. It is clear that the mind does not see itself as subject to a system of abstract norms. The only reality which can impose itself on the mind is one which surpasses it in the line of its own excellence, that is, of inwardness. But precisely that which causes the determination of laws as well as essences rightfully to impose themselves upon the mind will respect in them the truth and goodness of sovereign subjectivity. It is in this sense that heteronomy is constitutive of religion. But it is a heteronomy by which an autonomous subject freely submits itself to an order not of its own making, in which he pays homage to the expression of the Good that imposes itself absolutely on his behalf.

I understand Duméry's impatience with the idea of a determining structure which could impose itself upon freedom from
outside. Essences and norms are only ways by which the mind
which transcends them tends toward the One. But these essences
and these norms the mind does not give to itself, any more than
it gives itself to itself. It receives them, as it receives itself. And
religion is precisely this, not at first a movement of man toward
God, but a movement of God toward man, implying a tension
between the divine sovereignty and human freedom, a radical
dependence of being and action. Thus, for fear of seeing the human mind treat its own creations as divine realities, Duméry
comes out with a God so separated from the world, so foreign
from the world, that one wonders if he is still the God of religion.

Furthermore, it indeed seems that here there is a contradiction
in Duméry's thought between the emphasis that he places on the
transcendence of freedom in its relation to all determinations,
and on the other hand his conception of the whole as a hierarchy
of essences. This seems to be bound up with his rejection of the
ontology which has its ultimate basis in existence as such. The
primacy that he gives to the One over Being inevitably also gives
primacy to the opposition of the one and the many over the relationship of uncreated being to created being. Persons become
accidents of the eternal intelligibility, instead of the intelligible
subsisting only in contingent persons (*PR*, I, 83).

One may then ask if the reductive method exalted by Professor Duméry, pretending as it does to preserve transcendence, is
not in the last analysis a rational reduction that takes us back to
a God who is the principle of intelligibility. Duméry's great men-
tors, Plotinus and Spinoza, seem to make this apparent. But if
this is the case, then the problem is serious. For there is more
authentic religious content in the anthropomorphisms of Isaiah
than in all of Plotinus and Spinoza. It is the religious element
as something irreducible from the rational that is reduced to the
rational—reduced, that is to say, in this case eliminated. And
so we do not go beyond Husserl, but return to a position which
is well prior to the phenomenology of religions.

Duméry's reduction of religion to rational principles becomes particularly apparent in his critique of Christianity.
This critique comprises the greatest part of his work. We can
only praise him for having chosen the religion he knows best as

the object of his critique, and can only admire the loyalty with which he agrees unreservedly to submit Christianity to criticism. This is in the best tradition. What is somewhat regrettable is that, lacking information about the other religions, Duméry has understood Christianity as an expression which is typical of religions, whereas on the contrary it constitutes an exception. A more rigorous phenomenology, such as that of Wach or Eliade, would have permitted him more clearly to recognize its irreducibility.

The character of the Christian revelation, insofar as it is to be distinguished from other religions, is that it bears essentially on the historical interventions of God, of which the Incarnation is the most prominent. These facts are reported in the Scriptures in an unpolished form. But criticism ought to confine itself to this matrix. This is precisely the role of theology, which is the exercise of reason on this particular fact of the history of salvation, the rightful content of the Christian faith. But apparently Duméry does not admit this. For him Christianity is composed of a system of patterns and categories which must be reduced to the requisites of the human mind. It is just this reduction which is the task of the philosophy of Christianity.

Let us here quote the author:

The critical method can only be from the side of immanence. . . . The immanentist method claims that reason has jurisdiction over religion and because of that it keeps it in harmony with the other domains of life. . . . The argument from authority remains extrinsic to the arguments of reason. . . . The immanentist method implies the rejection of all particularity. It is opposed to the various attempts to limit the power of reason from without by the breaking up of human reality into separate areas of influence. It is a defense of rationality and of intelligibility. In this respect it honors an imperative which is one with philosophical demands [CR, pp. 50–51].

As for theology, it is "the science of salvation, not of speculative discernment or purely rational reflection." Furthermore, what the theologian will learn from the philosopher about the Trinity is its dogmatic import, its religious meaning, its soteriological value; he will not learn about its critical structuration, its formal coherence, or its judicative modality (CR, p. 110).

This conception of the relation between philosophy and theology seems barely acceptable. It makes of theology a practical science of salvation without speculative value; it is the philosophy of religion that affords a rational critique of Christianity, and it accomplishes this critique by pointing out in Christian dogmas the resolutions of the mind as it seeks to grasp the Ineffable One. We say on the contrary that the philosophy of religion, inasmuch as it has for its object a rational reduction, results in showing that the Christian data do not refer to a mental or spiritual function, but to the authority of a revelation. Its critique consists in establishing the rational legitimacy of this authority. But it is the domain of theology, which is a speculative discipline, to elaborate upon what is given in revelation by means of reason. Theology should examine the representations of religion not in terms of the workings of the mind but in terms of the demands of this revelation itself.

We mention at this point an expression which recurs continually in Henry Duméry's works. He asserts that his critique of religion applies only to religious representations and not to religion itself. But his aim really concerns metaphysics and is not just the critique of knowledge. He does not confine himself to representations or symbols of God and of the intelligible, but speaks of their very reality. These are determinate realities, not only because they are representations, but insofar as they characterize a sphere of existence, that of the intelligible, which he examines critically. Moreover, in the case which concerns us, these are no longer determinations of a dogmatic pronouncement, but the reality affirmed by dogma, as determination, of which he proposes the reduction.

Duméry applies this to different dogmatic statements. In *Critique et Religion* he criticizes Blondel for affirming that the revelation of the Trinity opens a path which is closed to pure reason. "This evades the difficulty. For it is a question of knowing how the notion of the Trinity is worked out. One cannot forget that it, too, took form by virtue of reason" (*CR*, p. 109). "The trinitarian system [consists] in applying a logico-metaphysical structure to quite diverse data. It involves a representation of the divine mystery by means of an ingenious supposition. Under these conditions it becomes evident that the mystery itself lies beyond this supposition" (*PR*, I, 201). Thus the Trinity constitutes a system which needs to be reduced. "God as mystery remains outside attainment" (*CR*, p. 109). And Duméry concludes, in a passage which so well betrays his thought,

"In order for the affirmed object to be valued from a rational point of view, it would have to harmonize with such a view. [Such is not the case here: the factual compounds with the ideal.] It remains for it to be found valid from the standpoint of religious behavior" (*PR*, I, 201–2).

Thus does Professor Duméry recognize the non-rational character of the Trinity. But instead of seeing there the expression of its suprarational character, irreducible to this rational proposition, that is to say, the appearance of a fact truly revealed, he sees there only the expression of an imperfect construction, which will demand further reductions and which has none but a pragmatic value. No one could say more bluntly that dogmas are pure determinations, created by the mind for approaching a mystery that remains inaccessible. And since they are created by the mind, the mind must see in them what it has wanted to put there, that is, schemes and categories, but without any speculative value.

Rational reduction, which Duméry uses to dissipate the reality of the Trinity as constitutive of the being of God, dissipates in the same manner the trinitarian events which constitute the economy and the design of salvation, the actions of sacred history. The idea of divine interventions in time is repudiated by our author. History rests upon a configuration which ought to be reduced. In reality the Christian affirmations of the Incarnation of the Word, of the Redemption as liberation from sin, of the procession of the Spirit, of the future Parousia, are mythical notions which should be reduced to their rational meaning. These meanings show those affirmations to be expressions of the eternal relationship between God and the mind.

The Christian affirmation consists alone in the unique character of the fact of Jesus. Here indeed is a factual datum which intervenes, and thus a historical movement. But this movement is only one of a progressive discovery of true religion, that is to say, of the fundamental relation of man and God. After the still crude patterns of primitive religions, after the progress accomplished by the Jewish people, in Jesus religion manifests itself in structures whose critical reduction shows that they express the inwardness and universality that are the requisites of the mind. Jesus is the religious summit of humanity. And this is why true religion defines itself by reference to him.

Duméry's position here reminds us of that of Bultmann. He also works a de-mythicization which is, in fact, as Cullman has shown, an elimination of history, and which implies in Christian affirmations—Incarnation, Resurrection, Parousia—the mythical expression of the man-God relationship. Yet the difference is that Bultmann does not try to reduce these expressions to a rational religion, but sees in them the expression of a situation of discontinuity. Besides, Bultmann seeks to disengage the fundamental Christian affirmation from representations and symbols which seem to him out of date. Here Duméry wisely remarks that the mind expressing itself as it must on all levels, cannot do without myths and that the evangelical myths are on the whole preferable to those by which one might wish to replace them (*PR*, I, 243).

Let us give some examples. That which we call the Incarnation is not a new event by which a new relationship is established between the Word of God and human nature. Theandrism is religion itself, that is to say, the eternal relationship between man and God, the presence of the One to the human spirit. But the Christ is the religious man in whom this relationship has found its perfect expression, in whom the intimacy between God and man which exists eternally is at last truly realized. "To believe is to rest on a series of facts (the history of Jesus) the affirmation of the intrinsic relationship of the human spirit to God. It is to affirm and declare that the attitude taken by Jesus has revealed the spirit of inwardness; it is to recognize that in the events of his life, the eternal mediation, immanent in the mind, is unveiled" (*PR*, II, 111).

Thus the Incarnation does not correspond to a new event, to an act of God. It is the representation of an eternal philosophical truth. How else would there be an act of God? For Duméry, the One is foreign to the world of determinate actions. He no more assumes them than does he create them. The idea of a divine intervention is unthinkable. Only human acts exist, and it is the mind that creates and invents. Its inventions are only the expressions of an intemporal reality. All history goes back to myth. Critical reduction has for its object precisely to disengage eternal meanings from their historical incrustation.

But all this we well know. Already this was the objection of Greek rationalism to the Incarnation. The idea that God came among men appeared as madness to Celsus and Porphyry. History was for them the world of the contingent and God the one who was a stranger to the contingent. Rationally, this is logical. And nevertheless, Christianity affirms that God became man. By the standards of reason this is pure folly. But the question is to know whether it is true. In every way this is an affirmation which cannot be reduced to the simple conception of a bond between the created mind and the uncreated One.

If we had to locate Duméry's position in relation to that of his master Plotinus, we would have to say that the sole difference is that for him Christian dogmas, which are only mythical representations of eternal truths, ought not be eliminated, but understood. Thus the integrity of Christianity is conserved. But it is conserved as the expression of philosophical truths on the imaginative level. The philosopher is one who knows that. He does not condemn the simple believer, who knows the truth but does not know how to examine critically the symbol through which he approaches the truth.

But does this not make the very content of the Christian affirmation disappear? Indeed so, for according to this affirmation the modes of God's presence in the cosmic religions, in Judaism, and in Christianity are radically distinct. To be sure, there are analogies between these modes of divine presence, and a phenomenology of religion is possible precisely because religions have analogous structures. But we must also respect the differences. In denying all intervention of God in history and in purely and simply assimilating the diverse modes of the presence of God, Duméry abolishes all phenomenology of religions.

Actually, the phenomenology of religions has as its basis a description which respects the data and their peculiar intentionality. It endeavors to establish an order. This is just what Joachim Wach did. Moreover, this order is not merely one of more or less happy formulations of universal data, but one of distinct data which are successive forms of one reality. We are thus led to a conception of one *Heilsgeschichte*, composed of separate events, but sustained by an intelligible unity among them. However, Professor Duméry does not do this, because his idealism refuses to recognize the objectivity of the divine actions which are the object of the Christian faith, objectivities which are irreducible to rational requirements and disconcerting for them.

One could easily show how Duméry applies the same method to the other events which constitute the object of faith. Take sin for example. The sin of Adam, which necessitated the redemption, is not a historical situation from which man can be delivered only by a redemptive action, but it is "man's mythical projection of his own guilt" (*PR*, II, 193). "This should be called noumenal. Ultimately this means that man can affirm himself properly only in recognizing his separation from himself, from God, and from others" (*PR*, I, 271). Thus original sin is a myth which must be reduced to a metaphysical meaning, that is to say, to the expression of a necessity which is constitutive of the life of the mind as such.

Consequently, exactly the same is true of the redemption. "It is not the event as event which saves," writes Duméry in referring to "Spinoza, who refused to enslave the mind to an idolatry of the historical. Exteriority could neither justify nor establish interiority. The latter in a rigorous sense can rest only on itself" (*PR*, II, 63). Consequently, the death of Jesus as such is only a *hapax*. We must reduce this to the operation which it signifies, which is both "internal and spiritual, as well as eternal, that is, to the mediation of the Word immanent in men's minds" (*PR*, I, 195). One will note the reduction of the *hapax* to the pure factitiousness of anecdotal history. It is not that Duméry ignores the opposition of *historia* and *Geschichte* (*PR*, II, 25), but *Geschichte* is for him meta-history, no longer history at all, but an expression of immanent necessity (*PR*, I, 271).

The notions of grace and faith, which Professor Duméry studies at length, would evoke similar remarks. Grace is the expression of the fundamental relation of man and God. It means that the mind can only realize itself by the immanent presence in itself of the One (*PR*, I, 283). This is the statement of a metaphysical truth which he puts in strong relief. But is it this ontological relationship that Christianity calls grace? Actually it denotes quite another thing, to have access to a participation in the life of the Trinity which surpasses absolutely the demands of the mind. But for Duméry this conception of grace is an idea which must be reduced to the necessary and immanent relationship between the mind and the One.

We find the same reversal of perspectives again and again. Whatever Christianity considers to be a gratuitous event, a free decision of the love of God, not reducible to the exigencies of the mind as such, is considered inversely as a mythical pattern which is merely the expression of an inferior level of needs constitutive of the life of the mind. So theology must be reduced to philosophy. But this amounts exactly to eliminating what constitutes the specificity of the Christian message, reducing it to a collection of myths—perhaps the most perfect myths, but ones to which philosophy alone gives us the final meaning.

One can say as much concerning faith. This is defined as the profound attitude of the religious man (*PR*, II, 38). It differs from purely rational procedure because "it embraces all the planes together," that is to say it expresses itself on the level of myths, of rites, of feeling, and also finally on the level of categories. But faith in the biblical sense is something quite different from the religious attitude as such. It is the adherence to affirmations which are irreducible to rational necessity and which derive their certitude from the authority of the revealed word. It is clear that this appeal to authority appears to Duméry as the strengthening of externalistic representations which should instead be reduced. But at once it is faith itself in its specificity that is eliminated.

This appears in a footnote where Duméry explains that "the *auctoritas Dei revelantis* is difficult to include in a phenomenology of faith" (*PR*, II, 148). The reason is that the action of the revealing God expresses itself in a sociological pattern, that of authority. This pattern seems too extrinsic, when we are dealing with the intrinsicality of truth or love" (*ibid.*). Here again, as always, Duméry seeks to disengage that which this pattern itself can express, which is divine truthfulness, the fidelity of God to himself. But this reduction would leave aside entirely the matter which is in question, not how to know the truth of God as the ultimate basis of all truth, but the fact of a historical revelation and of the devotion that the human spirit can offer it.

An examination of the results of Professor Duméry's critique on religion permits us to appreciate its value, but we must say that far from being an achievement in the phenomenology of religion such as Husserl, Van der Leeuw, Eliade, or Wach have conceived it, it runs the risk of compromising the results of phenomenology. Indeed, the thesis according to which religious representations are, like all determinate expressions, a manifestation of the creativity of the mind and thus referred ultimately to reason, fails to recognize the special contribution of phenomenology, which is the irreducibility of these representations to purely rational functions.

And so it rests that the problem posed by Professor Duméry concerning the systematization of the data furnished by the history of religions remains an essential problem. Even if the response which he brings to it is contestable, he does at least have the great merit of posing it boldly. On the other hand, by taking account in *Critique et Religion* of previous attempts at synthesis, he allows for the point about what may already be considered as dismissed and for the elimination of a certain number of false ideas which would compromise the research to which his books invite us. These are the positive results to which I should now like to return in order to sum up the main points. They make up the program which Duméry has proposed to us and which seems so clearly to express the present state of the problem.

The first task consists of clearing away certain inadmissible interpretations. Thus there is an entire order of "reductions" which are gotten rid of, the kind which the positivists of the nineteenth and early twentieth centuries delighted in making. Such are the attempts at explanations from social pressure or psychological sublimation. Duméry unmasks the fallacy of these interpretations in his treatment of the "naturalist prejudice." We must consider the "explicative methods" as insufficient "because their objectivism or their naturalism seeks to explain religion by something other than itself" (*CR*, p. 178). Likewise theories of a priori formations of religion, like that of Kant, are inadequate, "because their efforts at anticipation eliminate real religion and substitute for it a religion without a religious soul" (*Ibid.*).

Two fundamental premises thus seem to be dispelled. The first is the necessity of starting with "positive disciplines, especially history." It is here that the history of religions contributes a primary element. The error of ancient theodicies is indeed in having failed to recognize this positive substructure affording an immense mass of symbols, rites, and attitudes which form the data on which a reflection on religion may be carried out. The second premise is the recognition of the specificity of the religious fact. It is here that the contribution of phenomenology is decisive. Duméry makes much of this, whether it be a question of descriptive analogies like those of Otto in *The Idea of the Holy* or of a justification of these analyses by a critique of knowledge such as is suggested by the works of Husserl, Scheler, or Gabriel Marcel.

These results are already considerable. One may wonder whether Duméry does not in fact compromise them through his own attempts to surpass others, either in belittling the importance of the positive data through insufficient information or in compromising the results of phenomenology by a reduction which risks bringing us back to an immanentism of religious knowledge, which is really a transcendence of religious reality. But let us leave aside what we have already discussed. What is important for us here is the manner in which the problem is posed and the results which are considered achieved.

The problem with which one finds oneself confronted then, the same one which Duméry poses and which is actually the one which the science of religion faces today, is that of the organization of religious data in a coherent fashion. This consists of an effort to discern the meanings of the data furnished by the history of religions, to locate these different meanings in their proper relationships, and finally also to place various religions in their reciprocal positions with regard to each other. This last problem especially interested Joachim Wach. It concerns essentially the specificity of the Christian fact and previously the Jewish fact in relation to that of cosmic or non-historical religions. We have said that in fact Duméry sidetracks the issue, or more exactly, treats it in a deceiving fashion, neglecting the specificities and coming out with a purely relative and homogeneous hierarchy which admits only degrees.

On the other hand, in presenting the first two points of his program, he lifts up principles of great value and fecundity. In the first place it must be acknowledged that religious understanding cannot function except in terms of structures. This does not mean that these structures allow us to attain the transcendent itself. Duméry is a decided partisan of negative theology. God is always beyond all that we can imagine or conceive him to be. But conversely, what we conceive him to be really expresses something. Intentionality aims beyond the forms in which it finds expression, but in a sense it cannot go beyond these forms, patterns, or categories. It is of the nature of the human spirit both to aim toward God really and to aim toward him only through the finite forms of the mind.

In this manner Duméry dispels the illusions of those who would like to reject the forms of expression in order to get at a religious fact in its pure state. This is the illusion of the purely positivist exegetes. "The pure exegete would like, with the help of historical criticism, to make use of what has really happened, and consequently of what has been construed or imagined. In reality this choice is denied him" (*PR*, II, 24). Such is the fallacy of those who would recover a pure gospel prior to its interpretation in the structures of the Hellenistic mind. The Gospel has never been presented except through structures. But at first these structures were those of the world of the apocalyptics, and this was already a theology. This does not prevent religious reality from being attained, but it is always attained through representations which arise in the mind.

Such also is the illusion of kerygmatism,

. . . which claims to recover in its purity the first layer of facts and ideas which served as a point of departure for the first generation of Christians. 'Repristinizations' can only lead to a false primitivism. Kerygmatism already tends to be based on a first synthesis of facts and ideas. In no case does it rest on pure fact. It coincides with a certain cultural context which is not our own, but which is not the absence of all culture or of all interpretive superstructure. It is therefore vain to hope to recover a first gospel, stripped of all cultural envelopment. To lay bare the faith of our present mentality will always be to rediscover it in a mentality, never without one. The kerygmatic fallacy is to believe that faith was able to precede its cultural expressions [*PR*, II, 24].

It is in this same perspective that Duméry also rejects the demythicization of Rudolf Bultmann (*PR*, II, 243).

In the second place, Duméry's method is comprehensive, to the degree that it shows that religious reality is not apprehended only through certain special modes, but that it is expressed in myth as well as in concept. These modes of expression correspond to different levels of human expression, which is at once material, sensible, rational, and intellectual. Religious expression does not of itself reside in any one of these areas out of preference to any other. It is not a function of the imagination, as some would have it, neither is it a grasping by the intellect, as others see it. In reality God is transcendent over all these levels, although he can be approached through any of them. Religious expression therefore integrates and enhances the human being. And consequently it becomes possible to integrate all the aspects of religious expression into a single understanding. The only problem will be where to locate this understanding, and this will be the judicative element. This manner of proceeding appears to us as one of the most solid points of Duméry's thesis.

Here again Duméry's response is important. It sanctions first the rehabilitation of myths as authentic means of religious knowledge against a unilateral intellectualism. This appears as one of the essential results of the modern study of religion and of the convergence of the work of the historians of religions with the Jungian psychoanalysts and phenomenologists like Scheler. The truth value of feeling and image is here re-established. And consequently the whole immense contribution of mythologies and of mysticisms no longer appears as the residue of a prelogical mentality, but as the expression of a permanent structure of religious knowledge and understanding.

I am equally satisfied with Duméry's point that rational categories are a valuable and necessary means to knowledge of the holy. The biblical reaction against theology tends today in fact to devaluate as distortions the formulations and systematizations of the revelation in terms of Greek philosophical categories. There is a desire to return to a pure biblicism. Duméry denounces this as a fallacy. In the first place it ignores the fact that in the Bible the revelation is not in a pure state, but enmeshed in a mentality, and that the Semitic schemes are nothing but schemes. But above all, this view fails to see that the mythical expression corresponds only to an anthropological level and that conceptual expression constitutes a valid and necessary reduction.

In this respect Professor Duméry has good reason to criticize the unilateral position of Claude Tresmontant:

Even in making something special of the Semitic mentality, one must guard against attributing to it an exclusive primacy. . . . Minds like Clement of Alexandria, Origen, Gregory of Nyssa, and above all the Pseudo-Dionysus, believed, as Philo the Jew, that the Judaic and Greek cultures were more complementary than contradictory. One may ask, as the comparatists too often fail to do, whether the Jewish and Hellenistic cultures, by and large the Bible and Platonism, are not stages in an evolution more than they are conceptions of the world considered as complete and heterogeneous types of wisdom. Christian realism (more specifically, Judeo-Christian) is perhaps a permanent element of conscience; Greek idealism another level equally permanent [*PR*, II, 92–93].

These remarks are excellent. Their "comprehensive" conception links them with positions like those of Austen Farrer and Georges Florowsky. It guards against an anti-intellectualist reaction which would purely and simply be the suppression of one of the levels of religious expression. Moreover, their notion of a complementarity leads to an integral and hierarchical view of the contributions of diverse structures to religious understanding. One will note that here again Duméry limits his investigation to the Semitic and Platonic mentalities. It would be interesting to extend his method to other world views and to see if they would define other levels or at least offer some novel contributions.

In this domain, the books of Henry Duméry contribute incontestably principles which will serve to inspire the work of religious phenomenology. They will be recorded as the extension of the work of Wach, Van der Leeuw, and Eliade by their concern to go beyond the descriptive and to introduce a normative element. But we cannot say that they will go further. The new element that they would seek to bring, that of a philosophical reflection which would permit reference of religious knowledge to the dynamism of the mind and its grounding in the requisites of the mind, leads us back to a reduction which impoverishes the wealth of religious expressions and compromises their irreducibility.

MIRCEA ELIADE

Methodological Remarks on the Study of Religious Symbolism

I

As has frequently been noted, there has been for some time now a vogue for symbolism.[1] Several factors have contributed to the study of symbolism to give it the privileged place that it holds today. In the first place there have been the discoveries of depth psychology, especially the fact that the activity of the unconscious can be grasped through the interpretation of images, figures, and scenarios. These are not to be taken at their face value, but function as "ciphers" for situations and types which the consciousness does not want, or is not able, to recognize.[2]

Secondly, the turn of the century witnessed the rise of abstract art and, after World War I, the poetic experiments of the surrealists, both of which served to familiarize the educated public with the non-figurative and dream worlds. But these worlds could reveal their meaning only insofar as one succeeded in deciphering their structures, which were "symbolic." A third factor served to arouse interest in the study of symbolism. This was the research of ethnologists in primitive societies and, above all, the hypotheses of Lucien Lévy-Bruhl concerning the struc-

[1] Cf. Mircea Eliade, *Images et symboles* (Paris, 1952), pp. 9 ff.

[2] A clear exposition of the theories of Freud and Jung on the symbol is to be found in Yolande Jacobi, *Komplex, Archetypus, Symbol in der Psychologie C. G. Jungs* (Zurich, 1957), pp. 86 ff.

ture and functioning of the "primitive mentality." Lévy-Bruhl considered the "primitive mentality" to be prelogical, since it would seem to be ruled by what he called "mystic participation." Before his death, however, he abandoned the hypothesis of a prelogical primitive mentality radically different from, and in opposition to, the modern mentality.[3] In fact, his hypothesis had not encountered much support among ethnologists and sociologists, but it had been useful as a springboard for discussions among philosophers, sociologists, and psychologists. Furthermore, it drew the attention of the intellectual elite to the behavior of primitive man, to his psycho-mental life and his cultural creations. The present interest of philosophers in myth and symbol, especially in Europe, is due in large part to the works of Lévy-Bruhl and to the controversies that they provoked.

Finally, a considerable role in the vogue for symbolism must be attributed to the researches of certain philosophers, epistemologists, and linguists who wanted to show the symbolic character not only of language, but also of all other activities of the human spirit, from rite and myth to art and science.[4] Since man has a "symbol-forming power," all that he produces is symbolic.[5]

In recalling the most recent factors that have served to generalize and popularize the interest in symbolism, we have at the same time enumerated the perspectives in which the study of symbols has been approached. These are the perspectives of depth psychology, of the plastic and poetic arts, of ethnology, of semantics, of epistemology, and of philosophy. The historian of religions can only be grateful for these researches undertaken

[3] Cf. Lucien Lévy-Bruhl, *Les Carnets*, ed. Maurice Leenhardt (Paris, 1946).

[4] Cf. Max Schlesinger, *Geschichte des Symbols* (Berlin, 1912); A. N. Whitehead, *Symbolism: Its Meaning and Effect* (New York, 1927); W. M. Urban, *Language and Reality: The Philosophy of Language and the Principles of Symbolism* (London and New York, 1939); F. Ernest Johnson (ed.), *Religious Symbolism* (New York, 1955); *Symbols and Values: An Initial Study* (Conference on Science, Philosophy, and Religion, No. 13 [New York, 1955]).

[5] It is sufficient to recall the works of Ernst Cassirer, *Philosophie der symbolischen Formen* (3 vols.; Berlin, 1923–29) and his *Essay on Man* (New Haven: Yale University Press, 1944), and Susanne K. Langer, *Philosophy in a New Key: A Study in the Symbolism of Reason, Rite and Art* (Cambridge: Harvard University Press, 1942).

from different points of view on a subject so important to his own field. Since the sciences of man are interdependent, each important discovery has repercussions in neighboring disciplines. What psychology or semantics teaches us concerning the function of symbols is definitely of importance for the science of religions. Fundamentally, the subject is the same: we are always dealing with the understanding of man and of his situation in the world. A fruitful study might even be undertaken on the relationships between the disciplines mentioned above and the science of religions.

This is not to say that the field of the science of religions coincides with the fields of the other disciplines. Moreover, the very procedure of the historian of religions is not identical with that of the psychologist, the linguist, or the sociologist. It is just as dissimilar to that of the theologian. The historian of religions is preoccupied uniquely with *religious* symbols, that is, with those that are bound up with a religious experience or a religious conception of the world.

The procedure of the historian of religions is just as different from that of the theologian. All theology implies a systematic reflection on the content of religious experience, aiming at a deeper and clearer understanding of the relationships between God-Creator and man-creature. But the historian of religions uses an empirical method of approach. He is concerned with religio-historical facts which he seeks to understand and to make intelligible to others. He is attracted to both the *meaning* of a religious phenomenon and to its *history;* he tries to do justice to both and not to sacrifice either one of them. Of course, the historian of religions also is led to systematize the results of his findings and to reflect on the structure of the religious phenomena. But then he completes his historical work as phenomenologist or philosopher of religion. In the broad sense of the term, the science of religions embraces the phenomenology as well as the philosophy of religion. But the historian of religions *sensu stricto* can never ignore that which is historically concrete. He applies himself to deciphering in the temporally and historically concrete the destined course of experiences that arise from an irresistible human desire to transcend time and history. All authentic religious experience implies a desperate effort to disclose the foundation of things, the ultimate reality. But all expression or conceptual formulation of such religious experience is imbedded in a historical context. Consequently, these expressions and formulations become "historical documents," comparable to all other cultural data, such as artistic creations, social and economic phenomena, and so forth. The greatest claim to merit of the history of religions is precisely its effort to decipher in a "fact," conditioned as it is by the historical moment and the cultural style of the epoch, the existential situation that made it possible.

It is equally necessary to take account of the fact that theology is preoccupied essentially with historical and revealed religions, that is, with Jewish, Christian, and Muslim monotheisms, and only secondarily with the religions of the ancient Near Eastern and Mediterranean worlds. A theological study of religious symbolism will necessarily take into account selected documents from the great monotheistic religions rather than so-called "primitive" materials.[6] But the historian of religions aims to familiarize himself with the greatest possible number of religions, especially with archaic and primitive religions, where he has a chance to encounter certain religious institutions still in their elementary stages.

In brief, while the research on symbols in general and religious symbolism in particular by specialists in other disciplines deserves his consideration, the historian of religions is obliged in the final analysis, to approach the subject with his own means of investigation and in his proper perspective. There is no other perspective in which religio-historical data can better be integrated than that of the general science of religions. It is solely through timidity that historians of religions have at times accepted an integration proposed by sociologists or by anthropologists. Insofar as one can formulate general considerations on the religious behavior of man, this task rightly belongs to the historian of religions, provided, of course, that he master and integrate the results of the researches made in all the important areas of his discipline.

Unfortunately, this happens less and less frequently.[7] There

[6] Obviously, a theology of the history of religions will be obliged to take into consideration all these archaic and primitive religious experiences. But this theology presupposes the existence of the history of religions and depends on its results.

[7] Eliade, *op. cit.*, pp. 33 ff.

are few historians of religions who make an effort to follow the research undertaken in the domains which lie outside of their "specialty." If a historian of Greek religion at times take an interest in recent studies on Iranian or Indian religions, he is less inclined to follow the work of his specialist-colleagues, let us say, in Altaic, Bantu, or Indonesian religions. When he wishes to offer a comparison, or propose a more general explanation of phenomena of Greek or Mediterranean religions, he consults a "Manual," or pages through Frazer, or resorts to a current theory on the religion of the "primitives." In other words, he foils the very work which he is expected to do as a historian of religions: to keep himself informed about the research of his colleagues, specialists in other areas, assimilating and confronting their findings, and finally integrating them in order to better understand his Greek documents.

This hesitancy can be explained, it would seem, by two preconceived ideas. The first might be formulated in this manner: the history of religions constitutes a limitless domain which nobody can master;[8] hence it is preferable to know one area well instead of wandering like a dilettante through many. The second preconception, rather more implicit than overtly recognized, is that for "general theories" about religion it is more prudent to consult a sociologist, an anthropolgoist, a psychologist, a philosopher, or a theologian. Much could be said about the inhibition of the historian of religions who faces a work of comparison and integration. For the moment, it is important to rectify the erroneous opinion that exists concerning the task of integration.

It is not a question, for the historian of religions, of *substituting himself for the various specialists*, that is to say, of mastering their respective philologies. Such a substitution is not only impossible; it is useless. The historian of religions whose field of investigation is, for instance, Vedic India or Classical Greece, is not required to master Chinese, Indonesian, or Bantu in order to gain access to the Taoist religious documents, the myths of the aborigines of Ceram, or the rites of Tonga for use in his research. His task is rather to inform himself of the

---

[8] This is true of all the historical disciplines. More than fifty years ago Anatole France remarked that it would take several lifetimes to read all the documents concerned uniquely with the French Revolution.

progress made by the specialists in each of these areas. One is a historian of religions not by virtue of mastering a certain number of philologies, but because one is able to integrate religious data into a general perspective. The historian of religions does not act as a philologist, but as a hermeneutist. The mastery of his own specialty has amply taught him how to orient himself in the labyrinth of facts, where to go for the most important sources, the most appropriate translations, and such studies as are likely to guide his research. He endeavors to understand the materials that philologists and historians make available to him in his own perspective, that of the history of religions. It takes the linguist several weeks of labor to unravel the structure of a language with which he is not familiar. The historian of religions should be capable of arriving at similar results when working with religious data which are foreign to his own field of study. He is not held to duplicate the efforts of specialists, just as a historian of the nineteenth-century French novel is not expected to duplicate the labors on the manuscripts of Balzac or Flaubert, the stylistic analyses of Stendhal, or the research on the sources of Victor Hugo or Gérard de Nerval. His duty is rather to know about all these labors, to use their results, and to integrate them.

In like manner one can compare the method of the historian of religions with that of a biologist. When the latter studies, for instance, the behavior of a certain species of insect, he does not take the place of the entomologist. He expands, confronts, and integrates the investigations of the entomologist. To be certain, the biologist, too, is a specialist in one of the branches of zoölogy and benefits from long experience with such and such a zoölogical species. But his procedure is different from that of the zoölogist; he is preoccupied with the general structures of animal life, and not alone with the "history" of a particular species.

The second preconceived idea held by certain historians of religions, notably that it is necessary to consult another "specialist" for the total and systematic interpretation of religious facts, is probably explained by the philosophical timidity of many scholars. Two factors above all have contributed to implant and to foster this hesitancy: on the one hand, the very structure of the discipline which serves as a sort of introduction or preparation, to the science of religions (one knows that the majority of historians of religions are former philologists, archeologists, historians, orientalists, or ethnologists); on the other hand, the inhibition created by the lamentable failure of the vast theoretical improvisations of the end of the nineteenth century and the beginning of the twentieth (mythology considered a "disease of language," astral and naturist mythologies, pan-Babylonism, animism and pre-animism, etc.). Be that as it may, the historian of religions feels more secure if he leaves to other disciplines—sociology, psychology, anthropology—the risk of syntheses or of general theories.[9] But this amounts to saying that the historian of religions hesitates to complete his *preparatory work* as a philologist and as a historian through an effort of *understanding*, which, to be sure, presupposes an act of thinking.

II

It is not the intention of the writer to develop these observations touching on the field and methods of the science of religions. The purpose of this article is more modest. We want to show how we can envisage the study of religious symbolism in the perspective of the science of religions, and what the results of this procedure can be. In discussing this specific example, however, we shall confront methodological difficulties inherent in all research in the history of religions. To say this in another way, we shall have to discuss certain aspects of the method not *in abstracto*, but in such a way that these aspects may be grasped during the very process of research.

The first difficulty that faces the historian of religions is the enormous mass of documents, in our case, the considerable number of religious symbols. A problem is posed from the beginning: even supposing that one succeeds in mastering this mass of documents (which is usually not the case), has one the right to use them indiscriminately, that is, to group them, compare them, or even to manipulate them according to one's own convenience? These *religious* documents are at the same time *historical* documents; they are an integral part of different cultural contexts. To summarize, each document has a particular

[9] Indeed, all "general theories" which have dominated the history of religions from its beginnings have been the work of linguists, anthropologists, sociologists, ethnologists, and philosophers (cf. Eliade, *op. cit.*, pp. 35 ff.).

meaning, part and parcel of the culture and the particular time from which it has been detached.

The difficulty is real, and we shall endeavor later on to show how one can surmount it. For the moment suffice it to say that the historian of religions is destined to encounter a similar difficulty in all his work. For, on the one hand, he wants to know all *historical situations* of religious behavior, and on the other hand he is obliged to abstract the *structure* of this behavior, such that it can be recognized in a multitude of situations. To give but one example, there exist innumerable variants of the symbolism of the Cosmic Tree. A certain number of these variants can be considered as coming from only a few centers of diffusion. One can even admit the possibility that *all* the variants of the Cosmic Tree come in the last analysis from one single center of diffusion. In this case, we might be permitted to hope that one day the *history* of the symbolism of the Cosmic Tree may be reconstructed, by pinning down the center of origin, the paths of diffusion, and the different values with which this symbol has been endowed during its migrations. Were such a historical monograph possible, it would render a great service to the science of religions. But the problem of the symbolism of the Cosmic Tree as such would not thereby be resolved. Quite another problem remains to be dealt with. What is the meaning of this symbol? What does it *reveal*, what does it *show* as a religious symbol? Each type or variety of this symbol reveals with a particular intensity or clarity *certain* aspects of the symbolism of the Cosmic Tree, leaving other aspects unemphasized. There are examples where the Cosmic Tree reveals itself chiefly as the *imago mundi*, and in other examples it presents itself as the *axis mundi*, as a pole that supports the Sky, binds together the three cosmic zones (Heaven, Earth, and Hell), and at the same time makes communication possible between Earth and Heaven. Still other variants emphasize the function of the periodic regeneration of the universe, or the role of the Cosmic Tree as the Center of the World or its creative potentialities, etc.

We have studied the symbolism of the Cosmic Tree in several of our previous works,[10] and need not restate the problem here

[10] Cf. Eliade, *Patterns in Comparative Religion* (New York, 1958), pp. 270 ff.; Eliade, *Le Chamanisme et les techniques archaïques de l'extase* (Paris, 1951), pp. 244 ff.; and *Images et Symboles*, pp. 55 ff. and 213 ff.

in its entirety. Suffice it to say that it is impossible to understand the meaning of the Cosmic Tree by considering only one or some of its variants. It is only by the analysis of a considerable number of examples that the structure of a symbol can be completely deciphered. Moreover, one can understand the meaning of a certain type of Cosmic Tree only after having studied the most important types and varieties. Only after an elucidation of the specific meanings of the Cosmic Tree in Mesopotamia or in ancient India can one understand the symbolism of Yggdrasil or the Cosmic Trees of Central Asia and of Siberia. In the science of religions, as elsewhere, comparisons are made in order to find both parallels and distinctions.

But there is still more. Only after taking account of all the variants do the differences of their meanings fall into relief. It is because the symbol of the Indonesian Cosmic Tree does not coincide with that of the Altaic Cosmic Tree that the first reveals all its importance for the science of religion. Thus the question is posed: Is there, in either instance, some innovation, obscuration of meaning, or a loss of the original meaning? Since we know what the Cosmic Tree means in Mesopotamia, in India, or in Siberia, the question arises: Because of what religio-historical circumstances, or by what interior reason, does the same symbol in Indonesia reveal a different meaning? Diffusion as such does not solve the problem. For even if one could demonstrate that the symbol had been diffused from a single center, one could still not give the reason why certain cultures have retained certain primary meanings, whereas others have forgotten, rejected, modified, or enriched them. One can come to understand the process of enrichment only by disengaging the structure of the symbol. It is because the Cosmic Tree symbolizes the mystery of a world in perpetual regeneration that it can symbolize, at the same time or successively, the pillar of the world and the cradle of the human race, the cosmic *renovatio* and the lunar rhythms, the Center of the World and the path by which one can pass from Earth to Heaven, etc. Each one of these new valorizations is possible because from the beginning the symbol of the Cosmic Tree reveals itself as a "cipher" of the world grasped as a living reality, sacred and inexhaustible. The historian of religions will have to elucidate the reasons why such a culture has retained, developed, or forgotten a symbolic aspect of the Cosmic Tree. In so doing, he will be led to penetrate more deeply into the soul of this culture, and will learn to differentiate it from others.

From a certain point of view, one could compare the situation of the historian of religions to that of the depth psychologist. One, like the other, is obliged not to lose touch with the given facts; they follow empirical methods; their goal is to understand "situations"—personal situations in the case of the psychologist, historical situations in the case of the historian of religions. But the psychologist knows that he will not arrive at the understanding of an individual situation, and consequently cannot help his patient recover, except insofar as he can succeed in disclosing a structure behind the particular set of symptoms, that is, to the extent where he will recognize the main outlines of the history of the psyche in the peculiarities of an individual history. On the other hand, the psychologist improves his means of research and rectifies his theoretical conclusions by taking into consideration the discoveries made during the process of analysis. As we have just seen, the historian of religions proceeds no differently when, for example, he studies the symbolism of the World Tree. Whether he is led to limit himself, let us say, to Central Asia or Indonesia, or on the contrary proposes to approach this symbolism in its totality, he can accomplish his task only by taking into consideration all the important variants of the Cosmic Tree.

Since man is a *homo symbolicus*, and all his activities involve symbolism, it follows that all religious facts have a symbolic character. This is certainly true if we realize that every religious act and every cult object aims at a meta-empirical reality. When a tree becomes a cult object, it is not as a *tree* that it is venerated, but as a *hierophany*, that is, a manifestation of the sacred.[11] And every religious act, by the simple fact that it is *religious*, is endowed with a meaning which, in the last instance, is "symbolic," since it refers to supernatural values or beings.

One could say, then, that all research undertaken on a religious subject implies the study of religious symbolism. However, in the current terminology of the science of religions, the term "symbol" is commonly reserved for religious facts whose

[11] On hierophanies see Eliade, *Patterns in Comparative Religion*, pp. 3 ff. and *passim*.

95

symbolism is manifest and explicit. One speaks, for example, of the wheel as a solar symbol, of the cosmogonic egg as the symbol of the non-differentiated totality, or of the serpent as a chthonian, sexual, or funeral symbol, etc.[12]

It is equally common to approach a certain religious institution—initiation, for instance—or a religious act such as the *orientatio*, from the point of view of symbolism. The aim of such studies is to disregard the socio-religious contexts of the respective institutions of behavior in order to concentrate on the symbolism that they imply. Initiation is a complex phenomenon, comprising multiple rites, divergent mythologies, different social contexts, and heterogeneous ends.[13] In the final analysis, to be sure, all of this has to do with "symbols." But the study of initiation symbolism seeks another end: to decipher the implicit symbolism in such and such a rite or initiation myth (*regressus ad uterum*, ritual death and resurrection, etc.), to study each one of these symbols morphologically and historically, and to elucidate the existential situation which has made the formation of these symbols possible.

The same is true of religious behavior, such as in the *orientatio*. There are innumerable rites of orientation and myths that justify them, all of which are ultimately derived from the experience of sacred space. To approach this problem in its totality presupposes the study of the orientation ritual, of geomancy, of the foundation rites of villages, temples, and houses, and of the symbolism of tents, huts, houses, etc. But since at the root of all this lies the experience of sacred space and a cosmological conception, we can conceive the study of the *orientatio* solely as a study of the symbolism of sacred space.

[12] In like manner it is agreed that the term "symbolism" should be reserved for a structurally coherent ensemble; for example, we speak of aquatic symbolism, the structure of which cannot be deciphered except through studying a great number of religious facts which are heterogeneous in appearance, such as baptismal and lustration rites, aquatic cosmogonies, myths relative to floods or to marine catastrophes, myths featuring fecundity through contact with water, etc. (Cf. Eliade, *Patterns in Comparative Religion*, pp. 188 ff., and *Images et symboles*, pp. 164 ff. and 199 ff.). Obviously, the current usage of the terms "symbol" and "symbolism" lack precision, but one must accommodate himself to this state of affairs. In many cases the context suffices to clarify the meaning.

[13] Cf. Eliade, *Birth and Rebirth: The Religious Meanings of Initiation in Human Culture* (New York, 1958).

This does not mean that one should overlook or ignore the historical and social contexts of all forms of the *orientatio* that one has taken the trouble to examine.

We might give many other examples of this kind of research on a particular symbolism: the "magic flight" and ascension, the night and the symbolism of darkness, solar, lunar, telluric, vegetation, and animal symbolism, the symbolism of the quest for immortality, the symbolism of the hero, and so forth. For each of these examples the procedure is essentially the same. One should strive to grasp the symbolic meaning of the religious facts in their heterogeneous, yet structurally interlocking appearances; such facts can be rites or ritual behavior as well as myths or legends or supernatural beings. Such a procedure does not imply the reduction of all meaning to a common denominator. One cannot insist strongly enough that the search for symbolic structures is not a work of reduction but of integration. We compare or contrast two expressions of a symbol not in order to reduce them to a single, pre-existent expression, but in order to discover the process whereby a structure is likely to assume enriched meanings. In studying the symbolism of flight and ascension we have given several examples of this process of enrichment; the reader who wants to verify the results obtained by such a methodological procedure is referred to that study.[14]

III

The task of the historian of religions is not fulfilled unless he succeeds in discerning the function of religious symbolism in general. We know what the theologian, the philosopher, and the psychologist have to say on this topic.[15] Let us now examine the conclusions of the historian of religions as he reflects on his own documents.

The first remark that he is led to make is that the World "speaks" or "reveals itself" through symbols, not, however,

[14] Cf. Eliade, *Mythes, rêves et mystères* (Paris, 1957), pp. 133–64 (symbolisms of ascension and "waking dreams").

[15] We recall the analysis of Paul Tillich: "This is the great function of symbols: to point beyond themselves, in the power of that to which they point, to open up levels of reality which otherwise are closed, and to open up levels of the human mind of which we otherwise are not aware" (Paul Tillich, "Theology and Symbolism," in *Religious Symbolism*, ed. F. Ernest Johnson [New York, 1955], pp. 107–16).

in a utilitarian and objective language. The symbol is not a mere reflection of objective reality. It reveals something more profound and more basic. Let us try to enumerate the different aspects of depths of this revelation.

1. Religious symbols are capable of revealing a modality of the real or a structure of the World that is not evident on the level of immediate experience. In order to illustrate in what sense the symbol aims at a modality of the real which is inaccessible to human experience, let us recall a single example, the symbolism of water, which is capable of expressing the pre-formal, the virtual, and the chaotic. This is clearly not a matter of rational knowledge; rather does the living consciousness grasp reality through the symbol, anterior to reflection. It is by such graspings that the World is constituted. Later, as these manings expand, they will lead to the first reflections on the ultimate foundation of the World, i.e., to all cosmologies and ontologies, from the time of the Vedas to the pre-Socratics.

As to the capacity of symbols to reveal a profound structure of the World, we may recall what has been said above pertaining to the principal meanings of the Cosmic Tree. This symbol *reveals the World as a living totality*, periodically regenerating itself and, because of this regeneration, continually fruitful, rich, and inexhaustible. In this case also, it is not a question of a reflective knowledge, but of an immediate intuition of a "cipher" of the World. The World "speaks" through the symbol of the Cosmic Tree, and this "word" is understood directly. The *World* is apprehended as *life*, and in primitive thought, *life is an aspect of being*.

The religious symbols which point to the structures of life reveal a more profound, more mysterious life than that which is known through everyday experience. They unveil the miraculous, inexplicable side of life, and at the same time the sacramental dimensions of human existence. "Deciphered" in the light of religious symbols, human life itself reveals a hidden side; it comes from "another part," from far off; it is "divine" in the sense that it is the work of the gods or of supernatural beings.

2. This leads us to a second general remark: for the primitive, *symbols are always religious* because they point to something *real* or to a *structure of the world*. For on the archaic levels of

culture, the *real*—that is, the powerful, the meaningful, the living—is equivalent to the *sacred*. On the other hand, the World is a creation of gods or supernatural beings; to unfold a structure of the World is equivalent to revealing a secret or a "ciphered" signification of divine workmanship. For this reason archaic religious symbols imply on ontology. It is, of course, a question of a presystematic ontology, the expression of a judgment about the world and simultaneously about human existence, a judgment that is not formulated in concepts and which rarely lends itself to conceptualization.

3. An essential characteristic of religious symbolism is its *multivalence*, its capacity to express simultaneously a number of meanings whose continuity is not evident on the plane of immediate experience. The symbolism of the moon, for example, reveals a connatural solidarity between the lunar rhythms, temporal becoming, water, the growth of plants, the female principle, death and resurrection, human destiny, weaving, and so forth.[16] In the final analysis, the symbolism of the moon reveals a correspondence of mystical order between the various levels of cosmic reality and certain modalities of human existence. Let us note that this correspondence becomes evident neither spontaneously in immediate experience nor through critical reflection. It is the result of a certain mode of "being present" in the world.

Even admitting that certain functions of the moon have been discovered through attentive observation of the lunar phases (for example, the relationship with rain and menstruation), it is hard to conceive that lunar symbolism in its totality has been constituted by a rational process. It is quite another order of knowledge that discloses, for example, the "lunar destiny" of human existence, the fact that man is "measured" by the temporal rhythms illustrated by the phases of the moon, that he is fated to die but, quite like the moon which reappears after three days of darkness, man too can begin his existence anew, that in any case he nourishes the hope in a life after death, assured or ameliorated through an initiation ritual.

4. This capacity of religious symbolism to reveal a multitude of structurally coherent meanings has an important consequence. The symbol is thus able to reveal a perspective in which het-

[16] Cf. Eliade, *Patterns in Comparative Religion*, pp. 154 ff.

erogeneous realities are susceptible of articulation into a whole, or even of integration into a "system." In other words, the religious symbol allows man to discover a certain unity of the World and, at the same time, to disclose to himself his proper destiny as an integrating part of the World. Let us keep in mind this example of lunar symbolism. We then understand the sense in which the different meanings of lunar symbols form a sort of "system." On different levels (cosmological, anthropological, "spiritual"), the lunar rhythm reveals structures that can be homologized, that is to say, modalities of existence subject to the laws of time and of cyclic becoming, existences destined to a "life" which carries in its very structure death and rebirth. Owing to the symbolism of the moon, the World no longer appears as an arbitrary assemblage of heterogeneous and divergent realities. The diverse cosmic levels communicate with each other; they are "bound together" by the same lunar rhythm, just as human life also is "woven together" by the moon and is predestined by the "spinning" goddesses.

Another example will illustrate even better this capacity of symbols to open up a perspective through which things can be grasped and articulated into a system. The symbolism of night and darkness—which can be discerned in the cosmogonic myths, in initiation rites, in iconographies portraying nocturnal or subterranean animals—reveals the structural solidarity between precosmic and prenatal darkness on the one hand, and death, rebirth, and initiation on the other.[17] This makes possible not only the intuition of a certain mode of being, but also the understanding of the "place" of this mode of being in the constitution of the World and of the human condition. The symbolism of the Cosmic Night allows man to imagine what preceded him and preceded the World, to understand how things came into existence, and where things "existed" before they came to be. It is not an act of speculation, but a direct grasp of this mystery—that things had a beginning, and that all that preceded and concerns this beginning has a considerable weight for human existence. One has only to recall the great importance attached to the initiation rites implying a *regressus ad uterum,*

---

[17] It is equally necessary to add that darkness symbolizes precosmic "chaos" as well as orgy (social confusion) and "folly" (dissolution of the personality).

through which man believes he can begin a new existence, or the numerous ceremonials designed to reactualize periodically the primordial "chaos" in order to regenerate the world and human society.

5. Perhaps the most important function of religious symbolism—important above all because of the role which it will play in later philosophical speculations—is its capacity for expressing paradoxical situations, or certain structures of ultimate reality, otherwise quite inexpressible. One example will suffice: the symbolism of the Symplegades,[18] as it may be deciphered in numerous myths, legends, and images presenting the paradoxical passage from one mode of being to another, such as transfer from this world to another world, from the Earth to Heaven or Hell, or passage from a profane mode of existence to a spiritual existence. The most frequent images are: passing between two rocks or two icebergs that bump together continuously, between two mountains in continual motion, between the jaws of a monster, or penetrating and withdrawing unhurt from a *vagina dentata*, or entering a mountain that has no opening. We understand what all these images point to; if there exists the possibility of a "passage," this cannot be realized except "in spirit," giving this term all the meanings that it has in archaic societies, i.e., referring to a disincarnated mode of being as well as the imaginary world and the world of ideas. One can pass through a Symplegade insofar as one is able to act "spiritually," insofar as one proves that one possesses imagination and intelligence and, consequently, is capable of detaching oneself from immediate reality.[19] No other symbol of the "difficult passage"—not even the celebrated motif of the thin bridge like the blade of a sword or the edge of the razor to which allusion is made in the *Katha Upanishad* (iii, 14)—reveals better than the Symplegades that there is a mode of being inaccessible to immediate experience, and that one cannot attain to this mode of being except through renouncing the naïve belief in the inexpungeability of matter.

One could make similar remarks about the capacity of sym-

---

[18] Cf. Ananda K. Coomaraswamy, "Symplegades," in *Homage to George Sarton*, ed. M. F. Ashley Montagu (New York, 1947), pp. 463–88; cf. also Carl Hentze, *Tod, Auferstehung, Weltordung* (Zurich, 1955), esp. pp. 45 ff.

[19] Eliade, *Birth and Rebirth*, chap. iv.

bols to express the contradictory aspects of ultimate reality. Cusanus considered the *coincidentia oppositorum* as the most appropriate definition of the nature of God. But for many centuries this symbol had already been used to signify that which we call the "totality" or the "absolute" as well as the paradoxical coexistence in the divinity of polar and antagonistic principles. The conjunction of the Serpent (or of another symbol of the chthonian darkness and of the non-manifest) and of the Eagle (symbol of solar light and of the manifest) express, in iconography or in myths, the mystery of the totality or of cosmic unity.[20] Although the concepts of polarity and of the *coincidentia oppositorum* have been used in a systematic fashion since the beginnings of philosophical speculation, the symbols that dimly revealed them were not the result of critical reflection, but of an existential tension. In accepting his presence in the world, precisely as man found himself before the "cipher" or "word" of the world, he came to encounter the mystery of the contradictory aspects of a reality or of a "sacrality"that he was led to consider compact and homogeneous. One of the most important discoveries of the human spirit was naïvely anticipated when, through certain religious symbols, man guessed that the polarities and the antimonies could be articulated as a unity. Since then, the negative and sinister aspects of the cosmos and of the gods have not only found a justification, but have revealed themselves as an integral part of all reality or sacrality.

6. Finally, it is necessary to underline the *existential value* of religious symbolism, that is, the fact that a symbol always aims at a *reality or a situation in which human existence is engaged.* It is above all this existential dimension that marks off and distinguishes symbols from concepts. Symbols still keep their contact with the profound sources of life; they express, one might say, the "spiritual as lived" (*le spirituel vécu*). This is why symbols have, as it were, a "numinous aura"; they reveal that the modalities of the spirit are at the same time manifestations of life, and, consequently, they directly engage human existence. The religious symbol not only unveils a structure of reality or a dimension of existence; by the same stroke it brings a *meaning* into human existence. This is why even symbols

[20] Eliade, *Patterns in Comparative Religion*, pp. 419 ff.

aiming at the ultimate reality conjointly constitute existential revelations for the man who deciphers their message.

The religious symbol translates a human situation into cosmological terms and vice versa; more precisely, it reveals the continuity between the structures of human existence and cosmic structures. This means that man does not feel himself "isolated" in the cosmos, but that he "opens out" to a world which, thanks to a symbol, proves "familiar." On the other hand, the cosmological values of symbols enable him to leave behind the subjectivity of a situation and to recognize the objectivity of his personal experiences.

It follows that he who understands a symbol not only "opens out" to the objective world, but at the same time succeeds in emerging from his particular situation and in attaining a comprehension of the universal. This is explained by the fact that symbols have a way of causing immediate reality, as well as particular situations, to "burst." Whenever a tree incarnates the World Tree or when a spade is associated with the phallus and agricultural work with the act of generation, for example, one could say that the immediate reality of these objects or actions "bursts" or "explodes" under the irruptive force of a more profound reality. The same might be said of an individual situation, let us say, that of the neophyte locked up in the initiation hut. The symbolism "bursts" the bonds of this particular situation, making it exemplary, that is to say, indefinitely repeatable in many and varied contexts (because the initiation hut is likened to the maternal womb and at the same time to the belly of a monster and to Hell, and the darkness symbolizes the Cosmic Night, the preformal, the fetal state of the world, etc.). Consequently, because of the symbol, the individual experience is "awakened" and transmuted in a spiritual act. To "live" a symbol and to decipher its message correctly implies an opening toward the Spirit and, finally, access to the universal.

IV

These few general remarks on religious symbolism should, of course, be elaborated and refined. Since it is impossible here to undertake a work which would require a whole book, let us confine ourselves to two more observations. The first concerns what may be called the "history" of a symbol. We

103

have already alluded to the difficulty confronting the historian of religions when, in disengaging the structure of a symbol, he is led to study and compare documents belonging to different cultures and different historical moments. To say that a symbol has a "history" can mean two things: (a) that this symbol was constituted at a certain historical moment and that therefore it could not have existed *before* that moment; (b) that this symbol has been diffused, beginning from a precise cultural center, and that for this reason one must not consider it as spontaneously rediscovered in all the cultures where it is found.

That there have been symbols dependent upon precise historical situations seems indubitable in a number of cases. It is evident, for instance, that the horse could not have become, among other things, a symbol of death, before being domesticated. It is evident as well that the spade could not have been associated with the phallus, nor agricultural work homologized to the sexual act before the discovery of agriculture. In the same manner, the symbolism of the number 7 and, consequently, the image of the Cosmic Tree with seven branches did not appear before the discovery of the seven planets, which in Mesopotamia led to the conception of the seven planetary heavens. Moreover, there are numerous symbols that can be traced back to specific socio-political situations existing only in certain areas and taking form at precise historical moments, such as the symbols of royalty, of the matriarchate, or the systems implying the division of society into two halves at once antagonistic and complementary.

Since all this is true, it follows that the second meaning which the expression "history of a symbol" can have is equally true. The symbols depending on agriculture, royalty, the horse, and others were very probably diffused along with other elements of culture and their respective ideologies. But to recognize the historicity of certain religious symbols does not cancel out what we have said above about the function of religious symbols in general. On the one hand, it is important to note that although numerous, these symbols which are bound up with the facts of culture and thus with history, are appreciably less numerous than the symbols of cosmic structure or those related to the human condition. The majority of religious symbols reveal the World in its totality or one of its structures (night, water, heaven, stars, seasons, vegetation, temporal rhythms, animal life, etc.), or they refer to situations constitutive of all human existence, that is to say, to the fact that man is mortal, is a sexual being, and is seeking what today we call "ultimate reality." In certain cases, archaic symbols linked with death, with sexuality, or with hope for an afterlife have been modified or even replaced, by similar symbols brought in by waves of superior cultures. But these modifications, although they complicate the work of the historian of religions, do not change the central problem. To suggest a comparison with the work of the psychologist, when a European dreams of leaves of maize, the important fact is not that maize was imported into Europe only after the sixteenth century and thus became a part of the *history* of Europe, but that as an *oneiric symbol*, the maize is only one of innumerable varieties of the *green leaf*. The psychologist takes account of this symbolic value rather than of the historic diffusion of maize. The historian of religions finds himself in an analogous situation when he deals with archaic symbols that have been modified by cultural influences and events, for example, the World Tree, which in Central Asia and in Siberia received a new value by assimilating the Mesopotamian idea of the seven planetary heavens.

In sum, symbols linked with recent facts of culture, although they had a beginning in historic times, became *religious symbols* because they contributed to the "making of Worlds," in the sense that they allowed these new "Worlds"—revealed through agriculture, through the domestication of animals, through royalty—to "speak" and disclose themselves to men, revealing new human situations at the same time. In other words, symbols bound up with recent phases of culture are themselves constituted after the same manner as the most archaic symbols, that is, as the result of existential tensions and of ways of totally grasping the World. Whatever the history of a religious symbol may be, its function remains the same. A study of the origin and diffusion of a symbol does not release the historian of religions from the obligation of understanding it; it is for him to restore to it all the meanings it has had during the course of its history.

The second observation extends the first one in a way, since it bears on the capacity of symbols to become enriched in history.

We have just seen how, under the influence of Mesopotamian ideas, the Cosmic Tree comes to symbolize, with its seven branches, the seven planetary heavens. In Christian theology and folklore the Cross is believed to rise up from the Center of the World, taking the place of the Cosmic Tree. But we have shown in a preceding study that these newly attributed meanings are conditioned by the very structure of the symbol of the Cosmic Tree. Salvation by the Cross is a new value bound to a precise historical fact—the agony and death of Jesus—but this new idea extends and perfects the idea of cosmic *renovatio* symbolized by the World Tree.[21]

All this could be formulated in another manner. Symbols are capable of being understood on more and more "elevated" planes of reference. The symbolism of darkness allows us to grasp its meaning not only in its cosmological and initiatory contexts (cosmic night, prenatal darkness, etc.), but also in the mystical experience of the "dark night of the soul" of St. John of the Cross. The case of the symbolism of the Symplegades is still more evident. As for the symbols expressing the *coincidentia oppositorum*, we know what role they have played in philosophical and theological speculations. But then one may ask if these "elevated" meanings were not in some manner implied in the other meanings, and if, as a consequence, they were, if not plainly understood, at least vaguely felt by men living on archaic levels of culture. This poses an important problem which unfortunately we cannot discuss here; how can one judge how far these "elevated" meanings of a symbol are fully known and realized by such and such an individual belonging to such and such a culture?[22] The difficulty of the problem rests in the fact that symbols address themselves not only to the awakened consciousness, but to the totality of the psychic life. Consequently, we do not have the right to conclude that the message of the symbols is confined to the meanings of which a certain number of individuals are fully conscious, even when we learn from a rigorous investigation of these individuals what they think of such and such a symbol

[21] Eliade, *Images et symboles*, pp. 213 ff.; Hugo Rahner, "The Christian Mystery and the Pagan Mysteries," *The Mysteries: Papers from the Eranos Yearbooks* (New York, 1955), II, 337–401, esp. 380 ff.

[22] Cf. Eliade, "Centre du monde, temple, maison" in *Le Symbolisme cosmique des monuments religieux* (Rome, 1957), pp. 57–82, esp. pp. 58 ff.

belonging to their own tradition. Depth psychology has **taught** us that the symbol delivers its message and fulfils its function even when its meaning escapes awareness.

This admitted, two important consequences follow:

1. If at a certain moment in history a religious symbol has been able to express clearly a transcendent meaning, one is justified in supposing that this meaning might have been already grasped dimly at an earlier epoch.

2. In order to decipher a religious symbol, not only is it necessary to take into consideration all of its contexts, but one must above all reflect on the meanings that this symbol has had in what we might call its "maturity." Analyzing the symbolism of magic flight in a previous work, we came to the conclusion that it reveals dimly the ideas of "liberty" and of "transcendence," but that it is chiefly on the level of spiritual activity that the symbolism of flight and of ascension becomes completely intelligible.[23] This is not to say that one must put all meanings of this symbolism on the same plane—from the flight of shamans to the mystical ascension. However, since the "cipher" constituted by this symbolism carries with it in its structure all the values that have been progressively revealed to man in the course of time, it is necessary in deciphering them to take into account their most general meaning, that is, the one meaning which can articulate all the other, particular meanings and which alone permits us to understand how the latter have formed a structure.

[23] Cf. Eliade, *Mythes, rêves et mystères*, pp. 133 ff., esp. pp. 159 ff.

L O U I S   M A S S I G N O N

The Notion of "Real Elite" in
Sociology and in History

The useful and practical significance of the notion of "real elite" depends on the degree of reality ascribed to the individual person in relation to the group to which he belongs. Is the individual only one of a species, without his own originality? Such is the dictum of certain sociologists, for whom the real elite of a social group is but a chance product of statistical averages "standardized by repetition" (according to the conclusive judgment of Boltzmann). But such a statement robs this real elite of all its real qualities, for it identifies each of the members of this elite with the external relations in the hierarchical scale that differentiate it. Thus the personality of each one disappears and along with it the very usefulness of the notion with which we are concerned in this essay.

It seems to me, then, that sociology ought to go beyond this, and consider the notion of the real elite as an experimental resultant, obtained through investigations into group psychology. There is an inequality among men; a minority exists in every epoch and in every group. The cohesion of this minority has been sustained in a lasting and almost magnetic fashion by its "historical basis of reaction," its social vitality and action of persuasion. We read in Ecclesiastes of a certain person who suddenly showed himself capable of saving everything when the city was threatened, but fell back again into obscurity when the danger subsided. Posterity is grateful to them, to these superior men, these animators, pace-setters, inventors, and discoverers. They are the "great men" inscribed on Auguste Comte's universal calendar of positivism and, more recently, celebrated on the international calendar of UNESCO. But the cult of such men dies with the earthly cities which they have made flourish through some accidental invention (vanishing like the epidemic that it has wiped out) without much regard for their true personality. In truth, they have accelerated the process of disintegration by over differentiation (and "fission") of the cities and civilizations of this world. They have been able to "insensibilize" their bodies against the sufferings inflicted by disease but, in so doing, have hastened the decay of their spiritual support. It is true that some religions allude to "great souls." Hindus call them mahatmas, Arabians *abdâl*, and Christians saints, but they are usually ignored during their lifetime. And so, if their posthumous renown gives to their name a special glory, it is not because of their posthumous life, which spiritists and theosophists have not been able to establish with certainty, but to their apotropaion character. That is to say, they are not isolated in time but become part of a homogeneous series, bearing witness to the same certitude about the efficacy of spiritual means in improving corrupted social and political situations with their sense of compassion for the universal.

How does one establish this? How can one prove that every true human elite is apotropaion? In general, the historians pay very little attention to this. Our ordinary historical documentation comes almost entirely from a class of scribes, generally those concerned with fiscal matters, for whom the official praises of hired annalists are as suspect as the underhanded slanders of apocryphal memorialists. Play-by-play minutes of national parliaments, operational reports from headquarters of intelligence agencies, are worth no more than the caricatures and Pasquinades of "his majesty's opposition." And, as soon as the Marxist party seizes power, it manufactures an official history for political purposes which are even worse. Also a number of our philosophers of history, in their discouragement, reduce the unfolding of events to the mathematical application of an arbitrary axiomatic system of their own invention. Thus they explain the social upward mobility of the inner circle of Caesar or Napoleon in terms incomprehensible to the public of their times. This, in turn, is soon rejected by the founders of a new axiomatic system attempting to explain the evolution of humanity instead of seeking Jungian archetypes, the resurgence of which has coincided with the turning point of Caesar's or Napoleon's career.

The great attempt of Arnold Toynbee in his interpretation of world history does not escape the error of the axiomaticians. He has been reproached by sociologists for believing in the omnipotence of the scholarly analyst of the laboratory without ever having used the laboratory, and for explaining events as the function of "technical" expressions which hide reality from him in the same manner that the accounts of corporations are carefully edited and kept from the public by so-called "experts." No more convincing, and perhaps funnier, is the position of theosophy, which accepts the all-powerful synarchy, not that of the real elite of technicians, but of "those of the Agarttha" in their Tibetan *sous-sol*.

Let us return to the historians. In Semitic tradition, there is a strong tendency to reduce human history to an aesthetic number structure. The notion of real elite is for this tradition a simple fact of symbolic arithmology.[1] The *turba magna* of the Elect, in the Johannine Apocalypse is gathered up to the ONE by means of numbers: four (the four evangelical animals) and twelve (the twelve judges of the Twelve Tribes, the 144,000 Righteous Ones of Israel). The term *turba magna* itself refers to a people already thus classified, and their classification by number is based on the structure of their hierarchy. Islam, which best preserves the archaic elements of Semitic thought, has elaborated a very complete theory of the real elite, in is "numbered peoples."[2] It is not a case of people accidentally gathered on a *mosallä* (prayer esplanade) for similar gestures or chanting. It refers to a people whose concerted gathering increases until it reaches a collective number ("ordinal," rather than "cardinal," as A. Koyré suggested to the writer in 1932), attaining a Herbartian threshold, with a quantum qualifying it, reversing, as it were, a providential role. Through repetition

---

[1] "L'Arithmologie dans la pensée sémitique primitive," *Archéion* (Rome), July–August, 1932, pp. 370–71.

[2] "Exposé au Centre International de Synthèse" (Paris, 1932).

it consciously announces the "clamor for justice" (*sayhapil Haqq*) of its prophetic animator. For example, we are told that 'Umar was the thirty-eighth among the first forty adherents of Islam who dared to come out of hiding in a provocative manner. And still today, in a Syrian town when the number of initiated Nusayris reaches forty, they can and must found an initiation lodge (forty was also the number of the Martyrs of Sebasteia, who were the protomartyrs of the Greek order of Basilians). It is equally interesting to note that the number 313 is the number of the heroic elite selected by Gideon, and it also happens to be the number of victors in the first raid on Bedr by Islam. It is believed that in the supreme holy war the Mahdi will have 313 Companions.

Such symbolic numbers designate not only the simultaneous presence of the members in the group at a given time but also the duration in time of the groupings. According to the Koran (s. 18, v. 24), 309 is the number of years of the mysterious slumber of the Seven Sleepers in the Cavern of Ephesus, the time for their maturation by grace. It is also, for the Shi'ites, the period of the exile in hiding of the Fatimite pretenders up to the time of their victorious insurrection with their Mahdi in North Africa.[3]

This quantification of the span of human history would modify the Platonic conception in the *Timaeus*, making the history of the world a homogeneous and indefinite continuum, a simple reflection of the eternal return of the interlocking planetary cycles, with their conjunctions and oppositions. It would introduce into it a singularity, an irreversible progression, with condensations at its ritical moments, as individual points on a curve. This would form a fibrous tissue of typical events, in a structure of single or irrational numbers or in series, such as the Fibonacci series (1, 2, 3, 5, 8, 13, 21 . . .). As Bravais showed in constituting the science of phyllotaxy, this series really represents the rhythm of the vital growing of plant stems. The crises of growth, of parturition in pain (*ôdînes*), of humanity would coincide with the surging of the real elite from the mass in consciously substituting itself for the collective suffering, with the compassion reserved for the "royal souls";

[3] "Les sept dormants d'Ephèse," *Revue des Études Islamiques*, 1954, pp. 73 f.

111

I have noted this point with respect to the fate (and the vow) of Marie Antoinette, the last queen of France.[4]

The strong instinct for unity in Semitic thought is reflected in the undifferentiated character of the Arabic alphabet, which makes of each letter both the sign of a number and the element of a name. The method of aesthetic number is also an onomastic method. The Hijrian year 290, for example, corresponding to the year 902 of our Christian Era, evokes two feminine names of considerable eschatological importance in Islam, Maryam (mother of Jesus: $M + R + Y + M = 290$) and FATIR, the initiation name of Fâtima, daughter of the Prophet, ancestress of the Fatimites ($F + A + T + R = 290$). The coincidence of these two values meant for the Fatimite conspirators that the hour had come to revolt, since Maryam was going to "re-engender" Jesus for his triumphal return in the form of a Mahdi son of Fâtima, in whom the Spirit of Maryam in the Muhammadan cycle is revived. The revolt took place and led in the year 309 of the Hijra to the proclamation of the Fatimite Caliphate, which, incidentally, founded Cairo after Mahdiya.[5]

This instinct persists among non-Semitic peoples in the naming of newborn children. So that something of the elite of their dreams may pass into them, these infants are named after a war hero or a theatrical star, and it is believed that they will survive the rapid decline of their patron's glory, even though nothing of this glory may remain with them. Pierre Janet used to tell us that sociology can attain the real, provided that one applies a little psychological introspection, and this introspection can bring about a vivifying participation in other lives. In order to be conscious of themselves and to realize their destiny, the masses need to turn toward the names of transhistoric personalities, like the names of prophets invoked in the *recommandatio animae* borrowed from the Essenes by the Church of the Catacombs, a real elite if there ever was one. Frazer, in the "Dying God," and G. Dumézil in his researches on the first

[4] "Un vœu et un destin: Marie Antoinette, Reine de France," *Lettres Nouvelles*, September–October, 1955, Paris.

[5] *La Mubâhala de Médine et l'hyperdulie de Fâtima* (Paris, 1955); cf. also "La Notion du vœu et la devotion musulmane à Fâtima," extract from *Studi orientalistici in onore di Gioro Levi della Vida* (Rome, 1956), II, 1–25.

kings of Rome, have shown mistakes to which the scorn of this profound instinct can lead men, however basic it may be. And the investigations of parapyschology, like those of Gotthard Booth, have shown how "birds of a feather" gather in constellations of an ideal heaven, yet not without social efficacy.

An elite is necessary for introspection, the true moral relationship of the members to the whole body for the sake of the well-being of the group. In this regard Professor Bendick recently made a very interesting study of real elites in contemporary American society. He found it possible to show the exact bearing of someone emerging from such and such group into institutional life (executive, legislative, and judicial) on styles of dress or art of the different castes. Equally observable was the catharsis effected in these groups by their real elite, which heroically maintains what they consider the right scale of professional values against structural failures.

As a mathematician would say, there is no whole without a structure. In this view the structure precedes the whole, as quantity "fixes" the matter, whether it is a question of space or of time. A social body cannot be studied without introducing the idea of an operational group, or organic factor. It is the real elite which defends it against death. Without the hypothesis of the function of the real elite in such a group, at least latently, this cannot be understood.

But posing this philosophical hypothesis is not enough. We cannot grasp the notion of a real elite without recourse to an observation of human history. For example, there is a number, probably a fixed and limited number—archetypal, Jung would say—to which we can reduce the mass of themes in the universe as they might be catalogued by such folklorists as Aarne-Thompson. This limited number is that of dramatic situations endowed with a viable catharsis in a given social context. The elite becomes aware of these crises and finds in their outcome a recapitulation of its own definitive personality over and above the arbitrary schemes of philosophies of history. It is in such a heroic act that the elite affirms itself; an act endowed with an axial, communicative, and transsocial value, an act which is capable of raising the mass, of giving value to interested acts, as "in a series" (profitable virtues, mercenary acts, medi-

113

ocre appetites, leprous sins). The heroic elite is linked to these deeds only by its suffering in truly redemptive compassion for the universal.

Here I shall examine just one such act. Let us take the sacrifice of Abraham as an example. As a symbolic archetype this sacrifice has been recapitulated by Muhammad, the founder of Islam. It arises again and again throughout history in nocturnal ascension, found in the Christian sacrifice, the Table of the Sacred Host to console the Apostles for the departure of their Master (I Cor. 5:1–13). It can also be traced back through the Jewish Passover of the Exodus. It is noteworthy that the mystic Al-Hallâj wanted to become the ritual oblation in such a sacrifice. In assisting at 'Arafât at the dedication of the victim of the annual Hajj, he felt that the popular faith was waiting for the presence of a sole righteous one among the assistants, one whose unreflecting intercession might obtain general pardon for all the sins of the year. He wanted to take cognizance of this by compassion; and he was taken at his word.[6]

To which you may say to me: That happened a thousand years ago, are there still analogous cases? Yes, for in a real sense Gandhi was killed for the sake of justice, after a long exalted life, having taken upon himself all the pain and misery of the Hindu people.[7] In the person of this man of pain and suffering these people now recognize themselves. It little matters that after ten years this name should enter a momentary period of silence in India. In other countries, by an apotropaion substitution, the reflection of his torch has lighted other kindred souls. Thanks to the example of this old man grown thin by so many fasts and sacrifices, poised like a flaming target in front of the circle of suffering faces which his fire continues to light and to search out, the spiritual values of man are not defeated by the totalitarianism of nations.

[6] *Akhbâr al-Hallâj* (3d ed.; Paris, 1957), pp. 64, 161–62.

[7] "L'Exemplarité de Gandhi," *Esprit* (Paris), January, 1955.

ERNST BENZ

On Understanding
Non-Christian Religions

Joachim Wach was concerned with the historical and systematic study of the world's religions. The goal of his research was always the *interpretation* of religions, especially the non-Christian high-religions of Asia in their ethical and social, their liturgical and aesthetic, as well as their theological forms of expression. In one of his last articles, "General Revelation and the Religions of the World,"[1] he was still aiming to contribute to a better and more positive interpretation of religions on the basis of a new conception of "general revelation," and to press toward a profoundly theological understanding of the inner structure of the history of religions. He thus tended to reject what he felt was the "arrogance" of some Protestant dogmaticians in their judgment of the non-Christian high-religions as forms of a "human self-enfolding."

During the annual Eranos meetings in Ascona in the years 1951 to 1955, Joachim Wach often told me about the deep impression that the contact with the living forms of religious expression in modern Islam and Hinduism had made on him during his travels in Morocco and India. He emphasized repeatedly the enormous value of this kind of personal contact with the contemporary religious forms for the student of religion who ordinarily studies these forms only from literary documents belonging

[1] *Journal of Bible and Religion*, Vol. XXII, No. 2 (April, 1954).

largely to the historical origins or early classical epochs of those religions. In these conversations about the understanding of foreign religions we talked again and again about the difficulties confronting a Christian and a European in attempting to understand the non-Christian high-religions of Asia.

I was invited to be a guest professor at Doshisha University in Kyoto. At that time I had the opportunity to travel through the countries of the Middle East and the Far East, and I often remembered these talks during those years, as I came to learn about the many forms of religious expression in the Asiatic countries.

I felt I was well prepared for my experience in Asia. I had worked out lectures in English for the extensive teaching activity awaiting me en route. I was to lecture at universities in India, Ceylon, Burma, Thailand, and at my host university in Japan, as well as at numerous other Christian, state-supported, and Buddhist universities. For this task, I tried to orient myself inwardly for the intellectual and religious conditions under which I had to teach. I also acquainted myself with the professional literature of the science of religion concerning, especially, contemporary Hinduism, Buddhism, and Shintoism.

"Understanding" had not been a real problem to me during this time of preparation. From my ecumenical studies and works, I knew the various intellectual, liturgical, constitutional, and social forms of expression adopted by Christianity in the various churches and sects in the past and the present. I had studied with the Eastern Orthodox church for some decades, and visited its monasteries on Mount Athos, in Constantinople, in the Balkans, and in Russia from Kiev up to the Valamo Monastery at Lake Ladoga. For months I had lived in Orthodox surroundings. After these experiences I was confident that I would also find an inner access to the forms of religious life in Hinduism or Buddhism. Besides, my encounter with the Asiatic religions occurred under particularly friendly circumstances. I was guest at numerous Hindu and Buddhist centers and lived there in the community of teachers and students. For years before my arrival I had colleagues and friends in India and Japan with whom I had been in correspondence. Accompanied by my friends, I visited the sanctuaries and participated in the worship services and ceremonies of the various religions. With their sympathetic view and their

116

knowledge, they graciously explained to me the religious symbols of the temple and the forms of religious expression in the ceremonies. Discussions often followed my speeches or visits to the temples, and here I had an opportunity to ask many questions about these matters. While in Japan a serious illness forced me to a long stay in a hospital. This unfortunate experience, however, served to deepen my relationships with my colleagues and friends. After my release from the hospital, I was moved to find them even more willing to introduce me to the manifold and somewhat esoteric life of the various religions which existed side by side on Japanese soil. With all this experience, I thought I was in a favorable position to proceed with my work.

The problem of understanding, however, assailed me like an enemy. I had never anticipated how difficult the task of translation, for example, would be. While translating my own lectures into English, I realized how hard it is to reproduce in English theological concepts and religious experiences originally expressed in German. In translating my lecture on the history of Christian mysticism, I found it difficult to express in suitable English the experiences and thoughts of a Meister Eckhart or a Jacob Boehme. And how can one possibly express in English the meaning of the German *Geist?* All the terms available—spirit, ghost, mind, reason, reasonableness—prove to be inadequate. They imply at the most one single element of the complex German term *Geist*. More difficult still proved to be the attempt to translate ontological terms. In trying to give the different meanings of *sein, Wesen, Wesenheit, Wesenhaftkeit, Substanz, Essenz,* not to speak of translating terms like *Nichts, Nichtsein, Nichtigkeit,* and *Ungrund,* I met repeatedly with the adamant resistance of the English language. In the process of translating I found that the very structure of language itself seems to impede understanding.

But this difficulty of translation of one European language into another is a simple matter compared to the attempt to translate a European language into an Asiatic one. Since I myself didn't know any of the Eastern languages fluently, I was protected by my friends and hosts against some gross misunderstandings, for I always had the best interpreters at my disposal. I would always pass on to my interpreters the English version of my lectures so that they had the opportunity of becoming fa-

117

miliar with my material and preparing an adequate translation. Nevertheless, I repeatedly felt like the Rider on Lake Constance when I had read my English text and then listened to the interpreter delivering it in Singhalese, Burmese, Siamese, or Japanese. I had not the slightest possibility of controlling what he was telling my audience. Till the last day of my stay in Asia I never felt quite happy about this. In Japan, however, most of the interpreters were my friends, and I had the fullest confidence in them.

Some American colleagues, who had already experienced these difficulties, recommended a kind of test method. One such test was to insert a joke in the lecture occasionally. If the audience laughs when the joke is translated, the speaker may assume that the interpreter is doing his job faithfully. But even this rather crude method yields no certain proof among Asian peoples. Sometimes the audience smiles or laughs at points in the translation where in the original manuscript there is not the faintest cause for humor. Such experiences make a speaker feel so uncertain and so helpless that even the best "joke test" fails to reassure him. I have also had the opposite experience of telling an excellent joke which in the Japanese translation left the audience completely untouched. It was not noticed at all because the translator had not noticed it. Such experiences are apt to give the speaker an acute anxiety complex, to the extent that he completely doubts his ability to make himself understood.

One experience of this kind was impressed on me very deeply and painfully. I had been asked by the university of a non-Christian religious community, especially interested in the history of Christian missions, to give a lecture on the origin of Protestant missions in German Pietism and English Puritanism of the eighteenth century. In analyzing the foundations of this newly awakened missionary activity, I spoke on the idea of the Holy Spirit which had inspired the Puritan zeal for missions. I dealt especially with the concept of the new pouring out of the Holy Spirit as found in the theology of missions of Cotton Mather and other Boston Puritans. An interpreter was assigned to me, a young teacher who had just returned from two years study in America. He was considered an expert in English by his colleagues. I had a large audience and it was listening with the closest attention. During my lecture a friend placed a note on the lectern which read: "Your interpreter is not a Christian; he does not know the

Japanese word for 'Holy Spirit.' Please pass on to him this paper on which I have written the right Japanese term for it." There followed some Japanese characters. When I passed the paper on to him, he read it, nodded, and continued to translate, evidently using the new phrase. I never dared inquire what he actually made of the Holy Spirit in the course of my long treatment of it before the correction was made. The audience, at any rate showed no sign of a reaction. They listened to the conclusion of my lecture with the same silent attention as they had to the long first part. The introduction of the right word for "Holy Spirit" seemed to make no appreciable difference to them. This experience caused a kind of epistemological "seasickness" in me, and I had doubts even about Wach's theory of understanding. How many key terms in my lectures had been unknown to previous interpreters? How might they have improvised upon my carefully prepared lectures? May God pardon me and my translators!

In this connection I might mention that shortly after this I either completely revised my prepared lectures or threw them into the wastebasket, because I slowly began to sense how they might be received by my Asiatic audience. Theological education in Japan is patterned after German and Anglo-American models, yet it was impossible simply to read to Japanese students from a manuscript addressed to European listeners, because their assumptions about historical, philosophical, and theological subjects were so different. This became especially obvious with lectures on history. If one speaks to a European audience on Luther and the Reformation, one can assume at least a basic knowledge of the spiritual, cultural, and political background of the Reformation period. One can allude to certain generally known facts of the history of art or the life of the church and can count on invoking certain associations. This is impossible in Asia. The period of the Reformation, naturally, is foreign to the Japanese student, perhaps not intellectually but emotionally, just as the period of Shogun Hideyoshi is strange to a German student of theology. Or Peter Lombard is no closer to a Japanese student than Dengyo-Daishi is to our German student. To make the history of the Reformation intelligible to a Japanese student, means to explain it to him in terms of his own historical thinking and his knowledge of history and in positive or critical relationship to it; otherwise any such lecture remains incomprehensible. It takes an enormous effort and constant self-criticism for a speaker who wants to be really understood by an audience whose way of thinking is so different from his own. Most European and American guest professors have to resort to reading prepared manuscripts. One of my Japanese friends politely suggested that this is like setting off a firecracker. Sometimes the firecracker goes off and sometimes it proves to be a dud.

As I came to understand the essence of one non-Christian religion, it became at once increasingly clear to me to what extent and to what degree of depth our Western attitude, our intellectual, emotional, and volitional reaction to other religions, is modified by the European Christian heritage. It is one of the basic rules of the phenomenological study of religions to avoid judgment of other religions by criteria of one's own. However, I was repeatedly surprised by how difficult it is in practice to observe this rule. Our scientific-critical thinking, our total experience of life, our emotional and volitional ways of reaction, are strongly shaped by our specific Christian presuppositions and Western ways of thought and life. This is true even as regards the pseudo-forms, and secularized forms of thought and life, which are antithetical to the claims of Christianity. Indeed, we are frequently, in most cases even totally, unconscious of these presuppositions. Permit me to mention three points in this connection.

1. Our Western Christian thinking is qualified in its deepest philosophical and methodological ideas by a personalistic idea of God. This concept makes it particularly difficult to understand the fundamental disposition of Buddhism, which knows of no personalistic idea of God. The traditional Western reaction, in Christian theology as well as in Western philosophy, is to characterize Buddhist theology as "atheistic." It is difficult for a Westerner to comprehend the specifically Buddhist form of the approach to the transcendent. As for me, I had theoretical knowledge from my acquaintance with Buddhist literature, of the non-theistic tenets of Buddhism. But it became clear to me only when attending Buddhist "worship services," or in conversation with Buddhist priests and lay people. It is difficult for us to understand the non-theistic notion of Buddhism because the personalistic idea of God plays such a fundamental part in our Western logic. It took constant effort and new trials on my part

to realize that the basic difference between the two is not one of abstract theological concepts. It goes deeper than that, because this particular form of expression is attained by a certain training in meditation. It is here that the experience of the transcendent is cultivated and secured for the total life of Buddhism.

From Christian lecterns and pulpits we hear proclaimed in noisy and confident terms detailed information concerning the essence of God, the exact course of his providential activity and the inner life of the three Divine Persons in the unity of the divisive substance. But the reverent silence of the Buddhists before the "emptiness" of the transcendent, beyond all dialectic of human concepts, is pregnant with its own beneficence.

Buddhist art was the most important help to me in overcoming this intellectual "scared-rabbit" attitude toward the theological "atheism" of Buddhism. I was especially impressed by the representations of Buddha himself in the various positions of meditation. Our traditional theological ideas and concepts of God are a serious obstacle in understanding the Buddhist forms of transcendental experience. At best, Meister Eckhart's idea of the divine Nothingness, or Jacob Boehme's notion of the Non-ground (*Ungrund*) in God may serve as bridges of understanding from a Christian experience of the transcendent to a Buddhist one.

2. Hindu and Shinto polytheism confronted me with still another problem. I simply felt incapable of understanding why a believer preferred just one god or goddess among the vast pantheon. What attracts the wealthy can manufacturer of Kyoto to the shrine of the rice god Inari and causes him to donate whole pyramids of his cans and his pickles? I saw such offerings literally piled up beside other pyramids of rice wine casks and cognac bottles which other dealers had donated to the god of this shrine. In the Shinto pantheon of 800,000 gods this singling out of one of them was a real enigma to me. What moves the devout Hindu to pass by the Kali temple and the Vishnu temple on one day, and hurry to the sanctuary of Krishna to offer him his sacrifice of flowers and his prayers and to participate the next day in the Kali festival? In the mind of the devotee what role does the individual god play beside the other gods? Our understanding of all these problems is blocked by many factors. Consider for example the vigorous denouncements by the Old Testament prophets of

idols and idolatry among the ancients. Consciously or unconsciously, the modern Christian is influenced by such traditional attitudes. Nor can he fully appraise the strength of these attitudes if he reduces them to theological arguments. The battle waged against polytheistic practices by the Mosaic and Christian religions must be seen as a total emotional response which penetrates our attitudes more deeply than any intellectual affirmations.

Even the various European renaissances of classical antiquity have not appreciably changed this. We are still accustomed to seeing the ancient abode of the gods in the light of the poetic transfigurations of Humanism and Classicism. This whole world of gods defamed by Christianity, flares up once again in a kind of aesthetic romanticism. But these gods are for us at best only allegories. We are no longer able to imagine the religious significance that they had as gods for the faithful who prayed and sacrificed.to them.

In Asian lands, however, polytheism is encountered not as literary mythology, but as genuine religious belief and as living cultic practice. It appears in an overwhelming diversity and at the most varied levels of religious consciousness. As in the Hellenistic religions of late antiquity there occurred also in India a development toward monotheism. The Hindu deities Krishna, Vishnu, Kali, and others were worshiped as manifestations of Brahma, the one transcendental God, the Hindu God, much more reverently, however, than was the God of Plotinus, because the Hindu religion presupposes a plurality of worlds as over against the geocentric narrowing of the world picture of classical antiquity.

This development is the result of a profound change in the religious consciousness of India. In Shintoism, however, this change has not yet occurred. Its 800,000 gods have hardly been put into hierarchical order, each god being a particular manifestation of the Numinous by itself. While visiting Shinto shrine festivals, I often asked myself what moved the Shinto faithful to prefer this or that particular god, to sacrifice to him and worship him in a special way. (The shrines require rather substantial sacrifices after all state support has been withdrawn.) To seek the answer to this question in custom or convention in the relationship of certain occupational groups to certain deities is only to put off the question. Rather it seems to be the case that one worships the divine in such form as it has emerged impressively and effectively in one's own life, whether it be as helper, as bringer of luck, as protector and savior, or as a power spreading horror and awakening fear. It is the experience of the *numen praesens* which is primary and decisive for cultic devotion. Manilal Parekh, in his book on Zoroaster, puts this thought into an excellent phrase when he writes of the devotees of the Rig-Veda epoch: "They invoke a god because they need something from him, and for the time being he fills all their horizon. Thus it happens that there is no god who is supreme in this pantheon."

I asked my Shinto friends repeatedly: What is the essence of Shintoism in the veneration of the numerous gods at the various great and small shrines? One of them, a priest at a Shinto shrine, answered that it is the devotion to the creative forces in the universe in the bodily, the cosmic, the ethical, the intellectual, and the aesthetic realms. This answer doubtless meets the most important point. Decisive for this stage of the religious consciousness is the encounter with the self-realization of the transcendent in its individual form and expression of power. This encounter is the crucial factor, whether it occurs on a holy mountain or at a holy tree or fountain or in the meeting with an ethical hero. Correspondingly, the world of the gods is never finished; only the dead polytheism of our classic literary antiquity is "perfect," its Olympus complete, and philologically conceptualized. Living polytheism constantly creates new gods. One of the most important Shinto shrines is dedicated to the veneration of General Nogis, who in 1921 committed a demonstrative hara-kiri which was consummated in all the liturgical forms of religious self-sacrifice. By his act the dangers of Westernization were called to the attention of Japanese youth who habitually sense, recognize, and worship the transcendent in constantly new forms of appearances. It is precisely from Shintoism that in recent times there have emerged not only new gods, but also new religions. Living polytheism, therefore, is extraordinarily flexible and is open to systematization and a hierarchical organization. It is also capable of being accommodated to the various high-religions, as was the case in the monotheism of the Vedas, and also in Buddhism. Only Judaism understood the idea of the unity of God in the exclusive sense that all other gods beside Yahweh are "nothing." In the tradition of Jewish monotheism the Christian Church has used the exclusive interpretation of the unity of God to denounce the non-Christian gods of its neighbors as demons and to abolish their cults. Christian theology itself has screened the Christian doctrine of the Trinity, sometimes interpreted in a polytheistic sense, in such a way that the understanding of genuine polytheism was no longer possible.

3. The third point is that Hinduism, like Buddhism and Shintoism, lacks one other distinction so fundamental for our Christian thinking: the belief in the basic essential difference between creation and Creator. For our Western Christian thought this absolute discontinuity between Creator and creation is normative, but it does not exist in Buddhism and Shintoism. The same central importance that the idea of the absolute otherness of Creator and creation has for us, the idea of the unity of being has within Buddhist and Shinto thought. This idea of unity is connected not only with the particular method of direct religious experience, meditation and vision but also has a bearing on logic and conceptualization even where they are wholly unrelated to religious experiences as such.

Many other points might be mentioned in this connection, such as the relationship of man to nature, to the universe, and especially the idea of deification. It is baffling to the visitor from the West to note again and again how in the Eastern religions outstanding personalities are swiftly elevated to the rank of god, or recognized and worshiped as incarnations of certain divine attributes. This, however, only surprises one who holds the basic Western presupposition of the absolute discontinuity of divine and human existence. Viewed from the idea of the unity of existence, this step is self-explanatory just as the impassable gulf between Creator and creation is self-evident to us.

Another basic assumption which we hold as part of our Western Christian thinking is the common preference we attribute to theology, the doctrinal part of religion, when it comes to the interpretation of the forms of religious expression. But this preference is a specific sign of Christianity, especially Western Christianity of the Protestant variety. Whenever this viewpoint has been applied to the critical examination of Asiatic religions, an emphasis on their didactic and doctrinal elements has resulted. Thus, in interpreting Buddhism and Hinduism, some Western

124

authors have placed undue stress on their teachings and philosophy.

I myself was extremely surprised to find that in contemporary Buddhism, a much more central role is played by its liturgical and cultic elements. One element of religious life which has almost completely vanished from religious practice in Western Christianity, the exercise of meditation as a spiritual and ascetic discipline, is accorded a tremendous importance in Buddhism. This became clear to me only as I had the opportunity of seeing it first hand.

Meditation in Buddhism is not the privilege of a few specialists, but a practice directly shared by the majority of Buddhist lay people. To this day it is assumed in Buddhist countries that before taking over an important position in government, administration, science, or elsewhere in the social and military life, men must have undergone some training in meditation. Today it is still customary among many educated Buddhists to spend their vacations as temporary novices in a monastery and to give themselves to meditation. In Hinduism, too, meditation is still very much alive and is practiced in an astounding variety of forms and methods, because most of the great Gurus and founders of ashrams have developed their own form of meditation and Yoga and transmitted it to their disciples.

The importance of Eastern meditation has gradually been recognized in the modern Western literature on the science of religion and elucidated in various technical studies. However, the whole vast area of the symbolic language of Eastern religions as well of their liturgy and cults has hardly been noticed. I was surprised over and over by the power of the symbol in Buddhist worship services. Symbolic details were often explained to me by obliging priests. Especially in Buddhism does this symbolic language appear highly inaccessible. Above all, the symbolism of the movements of hands, arms, and fingers is very strongly developed. This hand and finger symbolism has in Eastern religions been brought to high perfection in two fields. It plays a role in the liturgical dances of India, where to this day a large number of symbolic hand and finger movements (*mudras*) have been preserved. It also figures in the practice of meditation and in the cult of two Buddhist schools, the Tendai and Shingon schools. Within the esoteric tradition of these schools, hand and finger symbolism was cultivated to an incredibly skilful and complicated system of expression which makes it possible to express through finger and hand symbols the whole content of the school's secret doctrine in one worship service. Just as significant are the symbolic positions of one's body, hands, and fingers during meditation. This is so because the person meditating puts himself into the position corresponding to the position of Buddha or some Bodhisattva on his way toward attaining full enlightenment.

It is often said that the religious life of Christianity is not confined to its teachings and its theology. This is certainly even more true for Buddhism, which, in essence, is practiced religion, practical meditation, symbolic representation, and cultic liturgical expression.

The Western Christian also must beware of transferring to the Eastern religions his own ideas concerning the organization of religion. We always assume more or less consciously the ecclesiastical model of Christianity when analyzing other religions. This approach suits neither Hinduism nor Buddhism nor Shintoism. The Japanese Buddhists do not form a Buddhist "church." Buddhism is, in fact, represented by a diversity of schools with their own temples and monasteries, and their own educational institutions and universities. These are not co-ordinated in any organizational fashion. Moreover, within the individual schools there is only a minimal organizational connection between the temples and monasteries. They are basically autonomous and economically independent units. A Buddhist federation was only very recently formed in Japan. This, incidentally, was inspired by the formation of the "Buddhist World Fellowship" in connection with the Sixth Buddhist Congress in Rangoon in 1954–56. But its concern is merely the representation of common interests among the different Japanese and Buddhist groups. It has nothing to do with ecclesiastical organization.

It would be equally misleading to apply to Eastern religions the idea that a person can be a member of only one religious community. This is a notion which stems specifically from confessional Christianity. It does not apply to Japan, nor to China, where in the life of the individual Taoism, Confucianism, and Buddhism mix and interpenetrate, as Shintoism and Buddhism do in Japan. The Japanese is a Shintoist when he marries since the wedding ceremony is conducted by the priest at the Shinto shrine; and he is a Buddhist when he dies, since the funeral rites are conducted by Buddhist priests, the cemeteries are connected with Buddhist temples, and the rituals for the souls of the dead are held in Buddhist temples. Between the wedding and funeral, the Japanese celebrates, according to private taste, preference, and family tradition, the Shinto shrine festivals and the Buddhist temple festivals. After the occupation, when the Americans took a religious census in connection with the religious legislation carried out by them, it was found, to their great surprise, that Japan, with only 89,000,000 inhabitants, registered 135,000,000 as the number of the faithful of all religious groups. In point of fact, there was no fraud involved. The curious surplus of religious adherents had resulted from individuals registering as members of both Shinto and Buddhist temple communities. For this reason they appeared twice in the religious census. The "Pure Buddhism" mentioned in our textbooks of the history of religions does not exist at all. For even in the various Buddhist centers of meditation and teaching, Buddhism is amalgamated with various levels of religious consciousness expressed in local mythologies.

I had occasion to attend the celebration of the consecration of a Buddhist priest. According to the ritual, the newly consecrated priest first offers his obeisance to the Sun-Goddess Amaterasu and afterwards to the person of the Emperor. This type of connection between Buddhism and Shintoism occurred in Japan as early as the eighth century. It followed from the teachings of Kobo-Daishi, who in his sermons taught the people that the Shinto gods are identical with the Bodhisattvas of the Buddhist doctrines. This identification occurred not only on the intellectual theological level, but on all levels of the liturgy, the cult, the religious symbolic language, and the mythology. It led to practical forms of conduct which cannot be judged by criteria of dogmatic thought and the division of religions on a doctrinal basis.

Another aspect of Eastern religions which was difficult for me to understand was that of magic and sorcery. I came into contact not only with exorcism and sorcery, but also with forms of magic in cultic dance, words, writings, and pictures. Here the Western Christian finds access to a wide dimension of religion otherwise completely barred to him by his own tradition. Christianity denounced the whole aspect of magic as "demonic" and banned it from the realm of Christian faith. This is just another of those surprising examples of how in Hinduism and Buddhism all levels of religious consciousness and all varieties of religion continue to exist side by side and to intermingle with each other. The European observer always feels himself pressed to create divisions and differentiations. Hindu friends of mine have observed that many European visitors interested in Hinduism ask the same question. Observing the devotion of Hindus in their temples, they ask How is it possible for such variant and mutually exclusive opposites to exist side by side in Hinduism? Together with the highest spiritual and ethical form of monotheism and the most elevated form of asceticism and of meditation, they are amazed to find such primitive sorcery and magic as might be seen in African fetishism. The Hindu's answer to this question will always be that such things are not at all mutually exclusive opposites, but represent stages in the development of religious consciousness.

There is a similar situation in Buddhism. Many of the cult rituals that I was permitted to attend were based on completely magical notions. I was particularly impressed for example, by the new year's service in a Zen monastery. On three consecutive days the festival of the so-called Daihanya, the physical turning-over of books, was celebrated. The basic idea of this festival is to set into motion the total content of the teachings of Buddha. But since this doctrine fills about 600 volumes, it is quite impossible for a small monastic community to recite it in its entirety in one service of worship. Such a recitation of the canon could only take place at an occasion such as the Sixth Council of Buddhism, where thousands of monks were occupied for a long period of time reciting the sutras consecutively.

Instead, at the Zen monastery, the spiritual moving of the content of the 600 volumes is magically accomplished by moving them physically. Piled on a low table in front of each monk are some ten to fifteen volumes of the canon. During the worship service each one of the volumes, written on a continuous folded strip, is unfolded like an accordion and folded again with a fluent ritual movement. The monk swings it briskly over his head while he calls out its title and first and last line. The idea is that through this physical motion the spiritual content of the books is actually set into motion. This liturgy counts as particularly meritorious, both for the liturgists themselves and for other Buddhists too.

For our Western thinking it appears absurd to set into motion the spiritual content of a book by liturgically leafing through it. We no longer have a sense for the meaning of magic, any more than for the difference between black and white magic. The peculiar basic assumptions on the relationship of spirit and matter underlying this idea are foreign to our thought and difficult for us to comprehend. These assumptions operate on a still more primitive level in the system of Buddhist-Lamaist prayer mills. This system consists of producing the spiritual content of a prayer through physical movements of the parchment on which the prayer is written.

It was equally difficult for me to understand the practice of sacrificing and its meaning. The ultimate emotional and spiritual motives for a sacrifice, the estimated value of a sacrifice, the enormous variety of sacrifices (sacrifices of flowers, incense, drink, animals, all with manifold liturgical and ritual variations) are extremely hard to fathom. This whole world is one which is largely closed to Europeans, especially to those of Protestant persuasion. It is a world to which we lost access centuries ago. The abyss separating us from the ancient idea of sacrifice cannot be bridged simply by an intellectual jump. There are, however, a few European philosophers of religion whose work is significant here. In studying the various types of sacrifice in the history of religions, Franz von Baader, for example, has been able to understand something about the mystery of sacrifice.

One other danger of misunderstanding lies in evaluating the mission of non-Christian religions. Here, too, Western observers are easily inclined to presuppose the Christian form of mission and propaganda, and its methods and practices among the non-Christian high-religions. Such assumptions can only lead to misunderstanding. It is true that a certain analogy exists between the expansion of Hinduism and Buddhism on the one hand, and the mission of Byzantium and of the Nestorian Church of the fifth to the tenth centuries on the other hand. The basis of mission here is not, however, a missionary organization, but the free and partly improvised activity of charismatic personalities who, as itinerant monks, counselors, and teachers, collected a group of

129

disciples around them. As a rule, this type of activity is related to the formation of monastic centers. In Hinduism we note the appearance of individual leaders who founded ashrams, and from these ashrams began missionary expansion or reform activity. In the same way the history of the expansion of Buddhism is most strongly connected with the appearance of such charismatic personalities. As itinerant preachers and founders of monastic communities, these men contributed their own particular forms of teaching and meditation. It has been only in very recent times that Buddhism adopted an organized mission activity. In this case, it is significant to note that the model for its methods of propaganda, as well as for its organization, is furnished by the organization and method of the Christian world mission.

Contrary to what may seem to be the case in this essay, my purpose here has not been to reproach or intimidate. I have enumerated some of these problems because I believe it is essential to clarify them if we would advance toward a better understanding of Eastern religions. Allow me to make a personal confession here in conclusion. What has repeatedly comforted me most in this work was the thought that we carry within ourselves the most essential condition for the understanding of other religions. In the structure of the human personality there is doubtless a tradition of earlier forms of religious experiences and of earlier stages of religious consciousness. Christian theology has succeeded in displacing most of these archaic ideas but has not been able to remove from our heritage those earlier stages of religious consciousness. Here in Germany, for example, we look back upon some thirty generations of Christian tradition. It goes without saying that the religious ideas and experiences of these generations were shaped in a more or less Christian way; but behind them lie, if mankind is really 6,000,000 years old as anthropologists have reason to assume, 180,000 generations whose religious consciousness has run through all the stages of animism and polytheism. It would be nonsense to assume that the experience of these early peoples has had no decisive effect on the spiritual and moral development of present-day mankind, as also on Christians of our own times. Somewhere in the bedrock layer of our religious awareness, the religious experience and various conceptual forms of our primitive forefathers live on. Somewhere in us also lies the heritage of the sibyl and of the haruspex; in some hidden corner we still harken to Pan's flute and tremble at the sound of the sistrum. Our aversion to horse meat is probably due to Christian influence, and is still not quite overcome. It lingers as a strong reminder of the sacred appetite with which our forefathers consumed the sacrificial horse thirty generations ago. We cannot separate ourselves from the experience and ideas of the countless generations behind us.

To Buddha in the night of his illumination under the bodhi tree was revealed the insight into all his earlier incarnations. For myself I covet another intuition: a clear insight into the earlier stages of the religious consciousness of mankind. I should like to know the way in which man has passed through these stages up to the present and how they lie submerged in the depths of our humanity in some form that is now barred and veiled from us. This is not the same as the desire to return to these stages. It is rather a wish to know the inner continuity of meaning in the development of the varied forms and stages of religious consciousness. And this desire does not seem to me to be non-Christian. For if history is in a sense the history of salvation, then this history cannot have begun with Moses in 1250 B.C. The history of salvation is as old as the history of mankind, which we assume is some 6,000,000 years older than Moses. And if this is so, then the history of religions and the history of the development of the religious consciousness must be seen as coterminous with the history of salvation. If the revelation in Christ is really the fulfilment of time, then it must also be the fulfilment of the history of religions. Then also, the earlier stages of religion which mankind passed through stand in a meaningful and positive relation to this fulfilment of time and of the history of mankind. On this basis, one of the most important tasks of contemporary Christian scholarship would be to set forth a new theology of the history of religions. The way would then be open to a real "understanding" among the religions of the world, as Joachim Wach envisioned it.

131

FRIEDRICH HEILER

The History of Religions
as a Preparation for the
Co-operation of Religions

"Have we not all *one* father? Has not *one* God created us? Why then are we faithless to one another?" These words of the prophet Malachi (2:10) were repeated several decades ago by a Jewish rabbi as he extended his congratulations to a Catholic bishop on the occasion of his consecration. The belief in *one* God should indeed awaken in the faithful among all the high religions the consciousness of belonging together in one family and their obligation to stand together fraternally. It is understandable that those who profess a divisive form of national polytheism should think of themselves as enemies not only for political reasons but for religious ones as well. National strife is for them also a war of their gods. But at first glance it seems inconceivable that those who profess faith in *one* God or *one* divine essence can combine with it a spirit of mutual estrangement and hostility.

But thus it has been in the history of religions. The faithful among the higher religions have opposed one another again and again, indeed if not engaging in bloody persecution, then despising the followers of other religions as deplorably ignorant persons who must be led with all possible speed to the true church and religion. How many human beings have become the victims of religious wars, how frequent the oppression of other religious consciences, how numerous are the martyrdoms suffered in courageous confession of individual faith! Think of the repeated instances of cruel persecutions of Buddhism by Confucianism in China and of Islam in India! Or of the outlawing of the Jews and their segregation into ghettos in the Christian Middle Ages, the ecclesiastical enforcement upon them of baptism and the attendance at sermons! Think of the Christian Crusades against Islam with all their brutalities, and in turn, the pressure of Muslim rulers upon Christian nations. Even in the religions familiar with the concept of tolerance, such as Hinduism, the converts to Christianity have been expelled from their families and castes and treated worse than pariahs!

Although in more modern times religious persecution has passed from the hands of religious to totalitarian political powers, the deeply irrational contempt for other religions is still widespread. Indeed in Western Christendom today it has in certain respects become more widespread than in the eras of the Enlightenment, Classicism, and Romanticism. When we think of the openness with which the Enlightenment philosophers welcomed Chinese philosophy (Schopenhauer's interest in Indian philosophy; Goethe's, Herder's, and Rückert's interest in Indian wisdom; Richard Wagner's and Friedrich Max Müller's interest in Indian wisdom),[1] we can understand Albert Schweitzer's lament of the present regression into narrow dogmatism, "We have a rich heritage from the past. This heritage has been squandered."[2] Those words appear increasingly appropriate when we think further of the progress of the study of the history of pre-Christian and non-Christian religions in the eighteenth and beginning of the nineteenth centuries. Evidence for this is Friedrich Meyner's *Allgemeine kritische Geschichte der Religionen* of 1807. Schweitzer's lament applies when we think of the enthusiasm with which a theologian like Friedrich Schleiermacher embraced

[1] Citations of Heiler: *Buddhistische Versenkung* (Munich, 1922), p. 68; "Um die Zusammenarbeit der Christenheit mit den nichtchristlichen Religionsgemeinschaften," *Schweizerische theologische Umschau*, XXII (1952), 3 f.; *Mitteilungen des Instituts für Auslandsbeziehungen*, V, Vols. I, II; "How Can Christian and Non-Christian Religions Cooperate?" *Hibbert Journal*, LII (January, 1952), 110. Cf. Ludwig Alsdorf, *Die deutsch-indischen Geistesbeziehungen* (Indian ed.; H. Vowinckel), 1942; Raymond Schwab, *Renaissance orientale* (Paris, 1950).

[2] Interview with Rudolf Grabs, Albert Schweitzer, *Denken und Tat* (Hamburg, 1952), p. 242.

133

the full diversity of the religious life of the non-Christian world in his *Reden*. Churchmen and theologians today are far behind that strong sense of unity that permeates the cultural work of UNESCO. If we ask why this sense of unity should be most hindered from that quarter where it ought be most vitally fostered, we will find the reason for this paradox in the sense of absoluteness characteristic of one segment of the higher religions.

In *An Historian's Approach to Religion*[3] (the best theological book of the last ten years, though not written by a theologian), Arnold Toynbee suggests that those three religions of revelation which spring from a common historical root—Judaism, Islam, and Christianity—have a tendency toward exclusivism and intolerance. They ascribe to themselves an ultimate validity. While the faithful among the Indian religions recognize the other religions insofar as they discern in them another manifestation of the essentials of their own religion, the three religions mentioned above (especially Christianity) are so exclusive that their followers often enough look upon other religions as the outgrowth of error, sin, and malice. Thereby they transfer the absoluteness which is an attribute alone of the divine and eternal to their own system of faith without seeing that this divine absolute can also be comprehended in entirely different forms of thought and devotion.

There is indeed something essentially correct in Toynbee's objection. The Indian religions are a treasure of more than two thousand years of tolerance. Two hundred and fifty years before Christ, King Asoka, one of the noblest figures in world history and the great promulgator of Buddhism, proclaimed to his subjects not only tolerance but also love for other religions. He states in one of his famous edicts carved in rock:

> The divinely favored King Piyadasi honors all sects, the ascetic as well as the local. He honors them with gifts and tributes of all kinds. But the divinely favored one does not lay so much weight upon gifts and tributes, but rather that in all religions there might be a growth in essence. The reason for this is that no praise for one's own religion or reproach of other religions should take place on unsuitable occasions. On the contrary, every opportunity ought to be taken to honor other religions. If one proceeds in this way, he furthers his own religion and renders good to other religions. Otherwise he does harm to his own religion and reproaches other religions, and all of this out of admiration

[3] Oxford University Press, 1956.

for his own religion. When he would magnify his own cause, he rather does all the more harm to his own religion. Unity alone profits, so that everyone will listen to and join the other religion.[4]

One will not find too many such admonitions in the history of the Christian religion. Yet among Christian theologians of all periods there have also been those who have noted the revelation of God in the non-Christian world. Thus Justin, the martyr-philosopher of the second century, stated: "All those who have lived by the Logos, i.e., by the eternal, divine World-Reason, are Christians, even if they have been taken as atheists, like Socrates and Heraclitus."[5] Thus Origen, who not only held the view that God had sent prophets to all peoples in all times but also admonished his fellow Christians to respect heathen forms of worship and sacred images. Thus Nicolas of Cusa, a cardinal of the Roman church, who perceived in all religions a longing for the one God.[6] Thus the Swiss reformer Huldreich Zwingli,[7] who believed all great heathens to be found in heaven—to Luther's consternation![8] Thus the spiritualists of the sixteenth century, above all, Sebastian Franck,[9] who confessed that God had spoken more clearly in such heathen personalities as Plato and Plotinus than through Moses. Thus Friedrich Schleiermacher, who glorified the great unity of all religions in his *Reden*[10] and affirmed that true Christianity is free of that drive toward exclusive rule and despotism.[11] Thus the Swedish Lutheran Archbishop Nathan Söderblom, who declared on his deathbed: "God lives, I can prove it by the history of religions." His posthumous work, treating the

---

[4] *Felsenedikt von Kalsi* (Corpus Inscriptionum Indicarum, Vol. I), *Inscriptions of Asoka*, ed. E. Hulzsch (Oxford, 1925), Vol. XIII; Moritz Winternitz, "Der ältere Buddhismus," in *Religionsgeschichtliches Lesebuch*, ed. Bertholet (Tübingen, 1929), pp. 151 f.

[5] *Apology* i. 46.

[6] *De pace seu concordantia fidei* (1453), ed. Faber Stapulensis (Paris, 1514), I, fol. CXIV b.

[7] "Expositio Christianae fidei," in *Werke*, ed. Schuler and Schulthess, IV, 65.

[8] *Kurzes Bekenntnis vom heiligen Sakrament* (1545, Erlangen ed.), XXXIII, 399.

[9] *Chronika, Zeitbuch und Geschichtsbibel* (1531); *Paradoxa* (1533), ed. Heinrich Ziegler (Jena, 1909); W. E. Peuckert, *Sebastian Franck* (1943).

[10] *Reden über die Religion*, Rede 5, p. 241, Centennial ed. of the original (1899), ed. Rudolf Otto (Göttingen, 1913), p. 123.

[11] *Ibid.*, p. 155.

principal types of the higher religions, bears the German title, *Der lebendige Gott im Zeugnis der Religionsgeschichte*.[12] And as there are such examples in Christendom, so also in Judaism and Islam there are pious men of thought who are free of exclusivism and who succeed in understanding the revelation of God in other religions. We may find examples among the Jewish Chassidim and the representatives of Reformed Judaism and also the Muslim Sufi of Arabia, Persia, and Turkey.

But Toynbee's reproach remains correct, that the majority of the representatives of the Christian church and theology are exclusivists and that many indeed look upon intolerance as a necessity and glory of Christian doctrine. The reigning tendency of current Protestantism, the so-called dialectical theology, denies every revelation of God outside the Christian Bible and looks upon the non-Christian religions as mere attempts at self-apotheosis which are under the judgment of God. One can hear such exclusivist theologians say over and over again that there is no communion between Christ and Belial, light and darkness, truth and deceit. They say there is no unity of gospel and religions, and a unity of religions is conceivable only in the sense of a perversion of all forms of extra-biblical piety, whether Christian or non-Christian.[13]

This gloomy picture of religions, however, does not correspond to the truth. Modern science of religion, analyzing the totality of the religions from their immediate living expressions in word, text, and art, shows us an entirely different perspective. Through the corporate efforts of various modern scientific disciplines such as philosophy, ethnology, prehistory and history, archeology, psychology, sociology, and philosophy, the methods of the science of religion have become increasingly broadened and refined. In this manner we are brought to a more comprehensive and profound view of religion and the religions than was possible in past generations, particularly those of the Enlightenment and Romanticism, which advanced so far in the science of religion. This study, in which scholars of greatest stature participated—men like Friedrich Max Müller, Nathan Söderblom, Rudolf Otto, Tor Andrae, Alfred Loisy, Gerardus van der Leeuw, Raffaele Pet-

---

[12] German ed. by Friedrich Heiler (Munich, 1942).

[13] Cf. Karl Barth, *Kirchliche Dogmatik* (Munich: C. Kaiser, 1932), I, 356 ff.

tazzoni—has given us a host of insights by which centuries-old prejudices have been removed.

The first impression conveyed by the study of the history of religions is that of the wondrous wealth of religions. That ancient saying, that awe is the beginning of philosophy, applies also to the science of religion. This sense of awe in the presence of the vast many-sidedness of religious phenomena permeates Schleiermacher's immortal *Reden über die Religion*, re-edited in its original form by Rudolf Otto in 1899 on the occasion of its centennial.[14] This sense of awe, however, is related not only to the fulness of religious forms, ideas, and experiences, which Schleiermacher described as "having developed out of the eternally provident bosom of the universe."[15] It is also related to the individual phenomena of the high religions now open to our spiritual world. Consider the enthusiasm with which Leibniz praised Chinese religion and philosophy,[16] the boundless accolade Schopenhauer heaped upon the mysticism of the Vedic Upanishads,[17] and the soaring hymn which August Wilhelm Schlegel[18] and Wilhelm von Humboldt[19] sang of that great mystic poem of Indian teaching, the Bhagavad-gita! With what devotion did Max Müller reveal to the West the beauties of the oldest bible of man, the Rig-veda,[20] and with what wonderment did Richard Wagner[21] and Anatole France speak of Gotama Buddha! And with what enthusiasm has Walter Eitlitz lately disclosed the miraculous

[14] *Reden*, Rede 10.

[15] *Ibid.*, Rede 5, p. 241.

[16] Quoted in N. Söderblom, *Das Werden des Gottesglaubens* (Leipzig, 1916), pp. 335 ff.; R. F. Merkel, "Leibniz und China," in *Leibniz zu seinem 300 Geburtstag*, ed. E. Hochstetter (Lief. 8, Berlin, 1952); also *G. W. von Leibniz und die China-Mission* (Leipzig, 1920).

[17] *Parerge und Parilipomena*, chap. 16, par. 184, Reclam V, pp. 418 f.

[18] *Bhagavadgita* (Bonn, 1823), pp. xxv f.

[19] *Schriften von Friedrich Gentz*, ed. Gustav Schlesier (Mannheim, 1840), V, 291, 300.

[20] "Lectures on the Vedas" (1865) in *Chips from a German Workshop* (London, 1867), I, 1–49; *Physical Religion* (Gifford Lectures) (London, 1890) (Leipzig: E. O. Franke, 1892).

[21] "Richard Wagner an Mathilde Wesendonck," in *R. Wagners Briefe in Originalausgaben* (Leipzig, 1913), V, 161; Pero Slepcevic, *Der Buddhismus in der deutschen Literatur* (Diss., Vienna, 1920), pp. 40 ff.; Günter Lanczkowski, *Die Bedeutung des indischen Denkens für Richard Wagner und seinen Freundeskreis* (Phil. Diss., Marburg, 1947).

world of Hindu Bhakti, i.e., love mysticism, to the Western world![22]

The second fruit of the religious quest is esteem for other religions. Hindus and Buddhists, Muslims and Mazdeans, Jews and Christians are filled with the same earnestness, sincerity, ardent love, obedience, and readiness to sacrifice. I shall ever keep before my eyes the deeply pious look of perfect devotion of two Muslim boys whom I watched at prayer in a Turkish mosque some years ago. Often enough Christians are put to shame by the deep piety, courageous confession, and active love for one's brother demonstrated in other religions. Thus did the fiery Florentine prophet Savonarola declare to his countrymen: "Jews and Turks observe their religion much better than Christians, who ought to take a lesson from the way the Turks bear witness to the Name of God. They would have long ago been converted, if they had not rightly been offended by the evil lives of Christians."[23] And in Lessing's *Nathan* we read the exclamation, "Nathan, Nathan, you are a Christian; by God, a better Christian there never was!"

More important than these initially direct and rather emotional impressions of other religions is the insight into the falsity of numerous polemical judgments of past times. Throughout many centuries the Christian polemic made Muhammad out to be a deceiver and paragon of baseness, until philological and historical inquiry moved him back into proper perspective and did justice to his religious genius.[24] The climax of several centuries of Islamic study is the work of a Swedish Lutheran bishop, Tor Andrae,[25] who clarifies with profound and devoted understanding even those features of the prophet which time and again had been the occasion of harsh judgment upon him. Hinduism had long been regarded as a confused and bizarre polytheism until study of the texts clarified the energy with which Indian theology comprehended the significant absence of duality, the unity of the divine beings, and the inwardness with which Indian

[22] *Die indische Gottesliebe* (Freiburg, 1955).

[23] Joseph Schnitzer, *Savonarola* (Munich, 1923), I, 258.

[24] Hans Haas, "Das Bild Mohammeds im Wandel der Zeiten," *Zeitschrift für Missionskunde und Religionswissenschaft*, Vol. XXXI (1916); Gustav Pfannmüller, *Handbuch der Islam-Literatur* (Berlin, 1923), pp. 115 ff.

[25] *Mohammed, sein Leben und sein Glaube* (Göttingen, 1932).

Bhakti mysticism embraced the redeeming favor of the one savior-god.[26] For decades Western theology was represented by the opinion that ancient Buddhism was nothing more than an atheistic world view and ethic which led to the nothingness of Nirvana,[27] until penetrating studies established that Gotama Buddha taught a mystic way of salvation leading up to the same supreme value which is the goal of all mysticism.[28] The great majority of arguments with which Christian apologetics thought to substantiate the falsity and inferiority of Eastern religions have been rendered untenable by scientific inquiry into the direct sources of these religions.

In displacing deep-rooted prejudices, scientific inquiry into religion has discovered more and more of the close relationship existing among outwardly differing religions. Innumerable parallels between Christianity and other religions have been discovered in recent decades by historians of religions. One really must say that there is no religious concept, no dogmatic teaching, no ethical demand, no churchly institution, no cultic form and practice of piety in Christianity which does not have diverse parallels in the non-Christian religions. Examples are the belief in the Trinity, in Creation, in Incarnation; the concepts of a virgin birth, vicarious suffering, the death and resurrection of the redeemer god; the inspiration of sacred scripture; the sole efficacy of grace; the forgiveness of sin; infused prayer; the imitation of God; the glory of paradise; the fulfilled kingdom of God; the priesthood and monasticism; sacraments and liturgical ceremonies, including the rosary. All these not only are Christian but are universally religious and universally human.[29] One needs only to consider the picture of the divine mother with her child as it appears to us from the dawn of time throughout the entire history of religions to the Madonna of the Far East—Kwan Yin, the Buddhist incarnation of mercy—and compare these with the

[26] Cf. esp. R. Otto, *West-östliche Mystik, Vergleich und Unterscheidung* (Gotha, 1926) (English translation: *Mysticism East and West*); "Vishnu-Narayana," in *Texte zur indischen Gottesmystik* (Jena, 1917, 1923), Vol. I, *Siddhanta des Ramanuja* (2d ed.; Jena, 1917, 1923); Eitlitz, *op. cit.*

[27] Heiler, *op. cit.*, p. 4.

[28] Cf. esp. Hermann Beckh, *Buddhismus* (Berlin: Göschen, 1919), Vol. II.

[29] Cf. Heiler, "Die Frage der 'Absolutheit' des Christentums im Lichte der Religionsgeschichte," *Eine heilige Kirche*, XX (1938), 318 ff.

Christian pictures of the Mother Mary and her child to realize that Christian and non-Christian humanity alike have knelt before one and the same image.

Non-Christian religions provide the student of religion with countless analogies to the central concepts of Christian faith and ethics; furthermore, the pre-Christian world of religion reveals itself to the student as the source and origin of definite Christian ideas, forms of doctrine, cultus, and organization. It is beyond dispute that postbiblical Christianity took over many elements from ancient metaphysics and ethics, the oriental-Hellenistic mystery religions, and the hermetic and neo-Platonic mysticism, and even from popular pagan piety and legal wisdom. This is precisely the great objection which Protestant theology has always had to Catholicism, that it has taken over so many pagan elements into Christianity. The Reformed theologian, Souverain, thought he had accomplished something great when in his work *Le Platonisme dévoilé*,[30] he unmasked the Platonic sources of patristic theology. But modern studies have shown that it is impossible, in view of the relationship of Christianity to the pre-Christian spiritual world, to make a sharp cleavage between the New Testament and later Christian literature. Historians of religions (Eichhorn, Alfred Jeremias, Gunkel, Gressmann, Bousset, Heitmüller, Clemen, Preisker, *et al.*) have revealed the intimate connection between the Old Testament and ancient oriental religion and between New Testament Christianity, late Judaism, and oriental-Hellenistic syncretism. Eissfeldt asserted: "The presuppositions and concepts of the history of religions have prevailed and become the common good of theological science."[31] A monumental witness to this assertion is the *Theologisches Wörterbuch zum Neuen Testament* by Kittel, in which the religious terminology of ancient Christian documents is interpreted through Jewish and Hellenistic literary sources. The two-volume work of the German theologian, Carl Schneider, which appeared recently, *Geistesgeschichte des antiken Christentums*,[32] shows that

[30] Published posthumously (1700); German edition (Loeffler, 1781, 1792); cf. Walter Glawe, *Die Hellenisierung in der Geschichte der Theologie* (Berlin, 1912).

[31] *Die Religion in Geschichte und Gegenwart*, ed. Friedrich Michael Schiele (Tübingen: J. C. B. Mohr [P. Siebeck], 1914), Vol. IV.

[32] (Munich, 1954), Vol. II.

early Christianity was thoroughly absorbed in an oriental-Hellenistic environment and that the entire early Christian thought and life was penetrated by Hellenistic thought and expressed itself in Hellenistic forms.

These variegated insights increasingly illumine that *unity* of religions that Schleiermacher intuitively grasped when he stated in his *Reden:* "The deeper one progresses in religion, the more the whole religious world appears as an indivisible whole."[33] And as the great Anglo-German scholar of religion, Max Müller, unceasingly proclaimed: "There is only one eternal and universal religion standing above, beneath, and beyond all religions to which they all belong or can belong."[34] Modern phenomenology of religion, represented primarily by the two Dutch scholars of religion, Van der Leeuw and Bleeker,[35] has confirmed this comprehensive unity by pointing out the similarities in the world of religious phenomena. The same was done by the psychology of religion with respect to the realm of religious experience[36] and by the sociology of religion, for which Joachim Wach wrote the classic work on the forms of religious community.[37] It is *one* bond that encompasses the lowest and highest religion. This unity becomes especially clear in religious language; the high forms of religion, the most subtle mystic, as well as the most vigorous prophetism, constantly speak the language of primitive magical religion without being conscious of it. Thus, for example, the primitive magical belief in blood and sacrifice, especially the belief in the atoning power of the υἰοθυσία, the sacrifice of a son, has become the form of expression for the deepest Christian mystery of redemption. The cultic δρώμενον has become λεγόμενον, the magic religious act surviving in the pious language of imagery.

Within the great unity spanning all religious forms and levels, the higher religions represent a closer unity. Although quite con-

[33] *Reden*, Rede 4, p. 186; ed. R. Otto, p. 95.

[34] *Leben und Religion* (Stuttgart, n.d.), p. 153.

[35] Gerardus van der Leeuw, *Phänomenologie der Religion* (Tübingen, 1933; 2d ed.; 1956); C. J. Bleeker, *Inleidning tot een phaenomenologie van den godsdienst* (Assen, 1934).

[36] Cf. Willi Hellpach, *Grundriss der Religionspsychologie* (Stuttgart, 1951).

[37] Haas, *op. cit.*; Pfannmüller, *op. cit.*

siderable differences exist between the mystic religions of redemption and the prophetic religions of revelation (and even among the latter there are great differences between the closely related Judaism, Zoroastrian Mazdaism, Islam, and Christianity)—important as these differences may be, they are overarched by an ultimate unity. There are seven principal areas of unity which the high religions of the earth manifest.

1. The first is the reality of the transcendent, the holy, the divine, the Other. Above and beneath the colorful world of phenomena is concealed the "true being": τὸ ὄντως ὸν, as Plato says;[38] the "reality of all realities" (satyasya satyam), "the one without a counterpart"[39] (ekam advitīyam) according to the Upanishads; "the eternal truth"[40] (alhaqq) in Islamic Sufism. Above all things transient rises the great cosmos, the eternal order, the Tao of ancient China, the rtam of ancient India, the Logos of ancient Greece. This reality is constantly personified in religious imagery as Yahweh, Varuna, Ahura Mazdah, Allah, Vishnu, Krishna, Buddha, Kali, Kwan Yin; it appears under the human imagery of the ruler, the father, the mother, the friend, the savior, the bridegroom, and the bride. The personal and rational elements in the concept of God, the "Thou" toward God, however, at no time exhaust the fully transcendent divine reality. They are only preparatory, in Rudolf Otto's beautiful image, "the Cape of Good Hope," the foothills of a mountain range which is lost to our eyes in eternal darkness.[41]

2. Second, this transcendent reality is immanent in human hearts. The divine spirit lives in human souls. The human spirit is, as Paul says, the temple of the divine spirit;[42] "God is nearer than our very pulse," as is said in the Koran.[43] He is interior intimo meo, "more inward than my innermost being," as Augustine said.[44] The ground of the human soul is identical with the all-pervading divine power; the atman is, according to the mysticism of ancient India, one with Brahman.[45] And the Christian

[38] Plato Republic vi. 490B.

[39] Bṛhad-Araṇyaka-Upaṇisad II, 3, 6; Chāndogya-Upaṇisad VI, 2.

[40] Reynold A. Nicholson, The Mystics of Islam (London, 1914), pp. 1, 81, 150 ff.

[41] Das Heilige, pp. 276 f.   [43] Koran, 50:16.

[42] I Cor. 3:16; II Cor. 6:16.   [44] Confessions iii. 6.

[45] Heiler, Die Mystik in den Upanishaden (Munich, 1925), pp. 23 ff.

mystics speak of the *acies mentis*, "the peak of the soul," with which it touches God; of "little sparks which issued forth from the Divine fire and glow within the human soul"; of the "birth of God in the ground of man's soul."

3. This reality is for man the highest good, the highest truth, righteousness, goodness, and beauty, indeed, extending beyond goodness and beauty, the "supergood," the "superbeautiful,"[46] as the Neo-Platonic mystics say, the *summum bonum*, the "highest good." This phrase is common to all mystics. We find it equally good in Lao-tse, Tao-teh-king, in the Bhagavad-gita, in the old Buddhist canon, in Plato, Plotinus, and among the Christian mystics.[47] There is nothing in the world of nature and the spirit to compare with this Ultimate and Supreme, this absolutely Perfect untouched by all transiency and darkness. Therefore, this highest good is the ultimate goal of all longing and striving of the high religions. "What is not the eternal," said Gotama Buddha, "is not worthy of man's rejoicing, not worthy that man should welcome it nor turn to it."[48]

4. This reality of the Divine is ultimate love which reveals itself to men and in men. Mercy and grace are the attributes of Yahweh in the experience of the prophets of Israel. The God of the gospel is outgoing and forgiving love. "God is love" says the Johannine parable.[49] Goodness and all-encompassing care make up the characteristic of the Tao of Lao-tse.[50] "The great heart of compassion" (*mahakaruna-cittam*) is the inmost essence of the Divine in Mahayana Buddhism,[51] and this heart is open to all men; just as the light of the moon is reflected in all kinds of water, the muddiest puddle as in the crystal-clear mountain lake and the endless ocean, so this divine heart of love reveals itself in all levels of mankind.

5. The way of man to God is universally the way of sacrifice. The path of salvation everywhere begins with sorrowful renunci-

[46] Plotinus *Enneadi* i. 8.2; vi. 9.6.

[47] Cf. Heiler, *Das Gebet* (Munich, 1923), p. 260; "Der Gottesbegriff der Mystik," *Numen, International Review for the History of Religions*, I (1954), 161–83.

[48] Majjhima-Nikaya, II, 263; Beckh, *op. cit.*, II, 123.

[49] I John 4:16.

[50] *Tao-teh-king*, 4, 25, 34, 52, 62.

[51] D. T. Suzuki, *Outlines of Mahayana Buddhism* (London, 1907), p. 292 and *passim*.

143

ation, resignation, the *via purgativa*, ethical self-discipline and asceticism. This path to God finds its continuation in meditation, contemplation, and prayer. Between contemplation and vocal prayer stands silent prayer.[52] In gesture and speech, prayer among the high religions compares to that of the primitive and ancient peoples.[53] The words of prayer in which human beings in need prayed to the Supreme Being thousands of years ago have survived to the present. But a change in content occurred in high religion. The exclusive, or at least central, object of prayer is God himself, according to Augustine, *Nolite aliquid a Deo quaerere nisi Deum*,[54] "you shall ask of God nothing other than God Himself," a saying quite similarly reiterated by the Persian-Islamic mystic, Sa'adi.[55] Insofar as human wishes were included in prayer, the object of the petition was liberation from all that separates from God, communion with God, and conformity of the human will with the Divine.[56] The prayerful cry, "Not mine, but thy will be done," has come from the lips of Christian as well as non-Christian men of prayer, ancient philosophers, and the pious men of Hindu, Buddhist, and Muslim religions.[57] And insofar as prayer is concerned with the whole world, it is the rule of God upon earth that is besought: *kšathra vairya* in Persian Mazdaism, *malkūth Jahve* in Judaism, the *basileia tou theou* in earliest Christendom.[58] All pious men pray, partly in words, partly without words, partly in complete solitude, partly in the community of the faithful. And the great saints of all high religions "pray without ceasing," as Paul says.[59] Their whole life is, as Origen said, "one single, great continuing prayer."[60]

In the last analysis, however, the prayer of the faithful is manifest not as the ascent of man to God but as a revelation of God in the heart of man. The greatest Islamic mystic-poet, Dschelāl-

[52] Heiler, *Prayer*, trans. S. McComb (New York, 1932), pp. 176 ff.

[53] *Ibid.*, pp. 40 ff.

[54] *Sermons*, 331. 4.

[55] F. A. D. Tholuck, *Blütenlese aus der morgenländischen Mystik* (Berlin, 1825), p. 241.

[56] Heiler, *Prayer*, pp. 180 ff., 241 ff.

[57] *Ibid.*, pp. 97 ff., 187 ff., 265 ff.

[58] *Ibid.*, pp. 248 ff.

[59] I Thess. 5:17.

[60] *De oratione* i. 12. 1; ed. Koetschen, p. 325.

ed-dīn-Rūmī, relates that a person who prayed almost came to doubt God because he received no answer from God to his prayer. Then came this message from God himself: "Your cry, 'O God' is my cry 'I am here'—in a single cry 'O God' are a hundred answers 'Here am I.'"[61] This faith reminds one of a word of God that Pascal believed he had heard: "You would not seek me if you had not already found me,"[62] and of the confession in Romans, "We do not know how to pray as we ought, but the Spirit himself intercedes for us with sighs too deep for words."[63] Because the eternal God himself is present in the soul of man as its secret ground, spirit, and spark, the soul creates a bridge between the finite and infinite by prayer and meditation. In this, too, all high religions agree, that their saints and devotees together form one great invisible chorus of prayer.

6. All high religions teach not only the way to God, but always and at the same time the way to the neighbor as well. A neighbor is not merely every man without exception, but every living being. The mystic way of salvation is not completed in the *via contemplativa*, in the "flight of the alone to the alone," as Plotinus said.[64] Rather it finds its necessary continuation in service to the brother, the *vita activa*. When Gotama Buddha had achieved perfect enlightenment under the bodhi tree, he withstood the temptation of remaining in undisturbed silence. Out of compassion for all beings perishing without his message of the way of salvation, he resolved to preach to all the sacred Truth disclosed to him.[65] Meister Eckhart declared that if someone in his highest rapture notices a sick man in need of a bit of soup, it would be better for him to leave his rapture and serve the one in need.[66] Confucianism, Taoism, Brahmanism, Buddhism, Hinduism, Mazdaism, Islam, and Christianity all preach brotherly love. The Buddhist canon contains a hymn of brotherly love, even as does the Christian New Testament. According to the

[61] *Mesnevi* III, 189 f. trans. Annemarie Schimmel.

[62] *Œuvres complètes*, I, 348.

[63] Rom. 8:26.

[64] *Enneadi*. vi. 9, 11.

[65] *Mahavagga*, I, 5, 2 f., *Majjhima-Nikaya*, I, 167 f.; trans. Hermann Oldenberg, *Buddha, sein Leben, seine Lehre, seine Gemeinde* (Stuttgart, 1914), pp. 139 f.

[66] *Reden der Unterscheidung;* Fr. Pfeiffer, *Deutsche Mystiker des 14. Jahrhunderts* (Göttingen, 1914), II, 553.

145

words of Buddha, all works of merit do not have one-sixteenth the value of love.[67] And we read in I Corinthians 13 that all the magnificent gifts of special grace are worthless and useless in comparison to the freely given, sacrificial, forgiving, and patient *agape*.

This love has no limitations. "As a mother protects her own child, her own son, with her love, so the disciples of Buddha have boundless love for all beings."[68] This universality of love finds its most wonderful expression in the formula of the Buddhist canon concerning the meditation on love, compassion, and mutual joy. The contemplative monk

lets the power of love, which fills his heart, spread throughout a heavenly realm, yea beyond a second, third and fourth realm, above, beyond, sideways, in all directions, in all completeness, he lets the power of love that fills his heart stretch out over all the earth. Such is the extent of that great, wide, and boundless love which is free from hate and malice.[69]

In like manner he radiates his compassion, joy, and holy equanimity throughout the entire cosmos. In its breadth and depth this meditation on love measures up to the universal intercessory prayer which is firmly rooted in Christian liturgies as well as in the individual prayer of the great Christian saints.

This love excludes no living being, it incloses even the sub-human creatures of the animal world. The Christian saints compete with Buddhist and Hindu saints in their love of animals. "St. Francis was a Buddhist," an Indian yogi once told me. One can just as well turn this around and say, "Buddha was a Franciscan."[70] The two currents of Christian love and Buddhist compassion for the cosmos flow together in the saying of one of the greatest Eastern Orthodox mystics, Isaac the Syrian, a saying that is at once entirely Buddhist and Christian:

What is a merciful heart? A heart inflamed for all creatures, men, birds, and animals, yea even for demons and all that is, so that by the recollection or sight of them tears fill the eyes because of the power of mercy which moves the heart in great compassion.[71]

[67] Ittivuttaka, 27; Winternitz, *op. cit.*, p. 83.

[68] *Sutta-nipāta*, 149; Winternitz, *op. cit.*, p. 84.

[69] *Digha-Nikaya*, XIII, 76 f. and other writings; Heiler, *Buddhistische Versenkung*, pp. 24 f., 79.

[70] On the parallelism between Buddha and Francis of Assisi, cf. Wolfgang Bohn, *Der Buddhist in den Ländern des Westens* (Leipzig, 1921).

[71] *Mystic Treatises by Isaac of Ninive*, trans. A. J. Wensinck ("Verhandelingen der Koninklijke Akademie van Wetenschappen te Amsterdam, Afdeeling Letterkunde," No. 23, 1), chap. 74, p. 341.

In later Mahayana Buddhism this contemplative love takes on a strongly active character. Love becomes the selfless service to all beings. "As the element of water brings growth to all grass, shrubs, and herbs, so the pure Buddha novitiate gives bud to all beings through the testimony of his love. He makes the good qualities of all beings grow."[72] The task to which he has dedicated himself in a solemn vow is the conquest of all suffering in other living beings through his own vicarious suffering. "I take upon myself the burden of all suffering . . . the salvation of all living things is my vow. . . . I must take upon myself the whole load of suffering of all beings. . . . I must bring the roots of the Good to maturity, so that all beings attain infinite happiness, unimagined gladness."[73]

One who becomes familiar with Buddhist lore is constantly struck by the purity, breadth, and depth of this love. But more astonishing still, this Buddhist love includes the love of the enemy, as also among Brahmans and Sufists. The early Christian writer Tertullian asserted that the love of the enemy was an exclusive characteristic of Christianity.[74] In this he was profoundly mistaken. All high religions of the earth, not only the Eastern religions of redemption but the pre-Christian religions of the West, know the commandment to love the enemy.[75] And the Chinese *Li-ki* (Book of Ceremonies) says, "By returning hatred with goodness, human concern is exercised towards one's own person."[76] The wise Lao-tse emphatically demands the "reply to adversity with mercy and goodness."[77] Loving the enemy has been commanded in India since the earliest times. We read in the heroic epic *Mahābhārata:* "Even an enemy must be afforded appropriate hospitality when he enters the house; a tree does not withhold its shade even from those who come to cut it down."[78] In the other epic, *Rāmāyana*, we read: "The nobleman

[72] *Kasyapa-parivarta;* Winternitz, "Der Mahayana-Buddhismus," in *Religionsgeschichtliches Lesebuch*, ed. Bertholet (Tübingen, 1930), p. 36.

[73] Vajradhvaha-Sutra in *Siksa-samuccaya*, pp. 280 ff.; Winternitz, "Der Mahayana-Buddhismus," *op. cit.*, p. 34.

[74] *Ad scapulam* 1.

[75] Hans Haas, *Idee und Ideal der Feindesliebe in der nichtchristlichen Welt* ("Leipziger Universitätsschrift" [1927]).

[76] *Li-ki*, 29, 12. Cf. R. Wilhelm, *Kungfutse Gespräche* (1921), pp. 164 ff.

[77] *Tao-teh-king*, 63; cf. 49.

[78] *Mahābhārata*, 12, 5528; O. Bothlink, *Indische Spruche, Sanskrit und Deutsch* (Petersburg, 1870–73), p. 573.

must protect with his life an enemy who is in distress or who out of fear has surrendered himself to the protection of the enemy."[79] Buddha admonishes his disciples:

Even if, O monks, robbers and murderers would sever one's members with a double-toothed saw, one by one, that person, if his spirit be filled with rage, would not be practicing my religion. Also in this case, then, you must beware: the mind must not be disturbed, we do not want to utter an evil word but remain kind and compassionate, well-intentioned, without inward hate; and we want to penetrate this human being with the spirit of goodness, with a boundless and immeasurable spirit free from hostility and ill-will.[80]

Buddhist literature contains wonderful examples of love for the enemy, as in the story of King Long-Sufferer, who, with his wife, was cut to pieces by the neighboring King Brahmadatta. Before his execution he admonished his son Long-Life: "Enmity is not pacified by enmity; enmity is pacified by peaceableness." When the boy at last had an opportunity to take bloody revenge upon the king who had brought such evil to his parents, he conquered all hatred through the remembrance of this admonition of his father.[81] Another example was Prince Kunala, whose eyes were torn out by order of one of the king's wives because of rejected love. When he was told of the commandment, he cried: "May she who issued this command through which such a salvation is coming to me, enjoy long life, happiness, and power." When the king wished to have the wife tortured and killed, he interceded, "If she has acted ill, you act well; do not kill a woman. There is no higher reward than that of love. . . . O king, I feel no pain, and in spite of the cruelty which has befallen me, I do not feel the fire of wrath. My heart bears only love for her who had my eyes torn out."[82]

The spreading of the concept of loving the enemy in pre-Christian times proves the validity of Lessing's statement, "Christianity existed before evangelists and apostles had written." But also post-Christian saints, Jews as well as Muslims, have preached and lived the love of the enemy. The Sufist

[79] Trans. A. Holtzmann, *Indische Sagen*, ed. M. Winternitz (new ed.; Jena, 1913), p. 292.

[80] *Majjhima-Nikaya*, 21; Karl Seidenstücker, *Pali-Buddhismus in Uebersetzungen* (2d ed.), p. 320; K. E. Neumann, *Die Reden Gotamo Buddhos aus der Mittleren Sammlung* (Munich, 1921), I, 352.

[81] *Mahavagga*, X, 2; Hermann Oldenberg, *Buddha* (Stuttgart, 1914), pp. 337 ff.

[82] *Divyavadana*, 405 f.; Oldenberg, *op. cit.*, pp. 340 ff.

Ibn Imad says: "The perfect man shall render good to his enemies; for they do not know what they do. Thus he will be clothed with the qualities of God, for God always does good to his enemies even though they do not know him."[83] The Jewish Chassidim also demand:

In humility, the pious believer shall not return evil for evil, but forgive those who hate and persecute him, and also love sinners. He shall say to himself, that in the eyes of God the sinner counts as much as he himself. How can one hate him whom God loves?[84]

These Jewish sayings ring like an echo of the words of Jesus in the Sermon on the Mount, "Love your enemies" (Matt. 5:44).

The faith that God is love and the commandment that men shall become like God in this all-embracing love, which includes enemies, constitute by themselves alone a strong sense of community among all high religions. The concept of humanity is basically no mere rational or purely ethical idea, but a deeply religious one. We of the West inherited this idea from the ethics of the Greek and Hellenistic religion, as well as from the prophetism of Israel whence came early Christianity.[85] But the Eastern cultures, too, have arrived at the idea of humanity by way of their religions. Confucius said: "All men dwelling between the four oceans of the world are brothers of noble men."[86] The corollary of the concept of humanity is the idea of universal peace. Lao-tse and his disciples appeared in China as mankind's first apostles of peace. Of the latter, a saying traditionally attributed to Tswang-tse says: "Through burning love they sought to unite fraternally the people of the world. . . . They forbade aggression and ordered weapons to be laid aside so that mankind might be rescued from war. . . . With this teaching they spread over the entire world."[87] In a Mahayanist writing it is said of the Buddha novitiates:

[83] Tor Andrae *Die Person Mohammeds in Lehre und Glauben seiner Gemeinde* (Uppsala, 1918), p. 223.

[84] Paul Levertoff, *Die religiose Denkweise der Chassidim nach den Quellen dargestellt* (Leipzig, 1918) p. 89.

[85] Cf. Heiler, "Die Bedeutung der Religionen für die Entwicklung des Menschheits—und Friedensgedankens," *Oekumenische Einheit*, II, No. 1, 1–29.

[86] Kung-tse, *Gespräche* (Lun yü), XII, 5; trans. Richard Wilhelm (Jena, 1921), p. 121.

[87] *The Texts of Taoism*, trans. James Legge, *Sacred Books of the East*, XL, 222; Richard Wilhelm, *Dschuang Dsi: Das Buch von südlichen Blütenland* (Jena, 1940), pp. xix f.

149

During the time interval of the ages, while men battle with weapons, their minds are directed toward love, and they exhort the hundred million living things to peaceableness. And in the middle of a great battle, the strong Buddha novitiates are equal toward all parties and advocate only peace and concord.[88]

Love is God's doing. It flows not from the small heart of man but from the eternal love of God. But as love flows forth from the heart of God, so it flows back to him again; the neighbor to whom man renders love is God himself in human disclosure. The ancient Greeks spoke of Zeus secretly approaching us in the stranger, the suppliant, the fugitive, and the companion, as Zeus *xenios, physios, hikesios,* and *metoikios.*[89] Buddha taught his disciples to care for him even in the form of his sick companions.[90] According to Jesus' prophecy of judgment (Matt. 25:31 ff.) the messianic judge will count every act of charity rendered to the hungry, thirsty, stranger, naked, sick, and imprisoned as done unto him and every such person neglected as the neglect of him, a thought briefly and concisely summarized by the extra-canonical saying of Jesus, "If you have seen your brother, you have seen your Lord."[91] Great founders of Christian monastic orders, men like Benedict, Francis of Assisi, and Vincent DePaul, produced wonderful variations of this idea.[92] In his preaching, Luther never tires of having his listeners learn that Christ ceaselessly encounters us in all beggars and those seeking help.[93] "The world is full, full of God, in every lane, at your door you find Christ."[94] *Homo homini Deus*—man in need is God in disguise and his permanent incarnation. "Here is thy footstool, there do thy feet rest where the poorest and lowliest, where the lost do live," is the prayer of Rabindranath Tagore.[95] Where there is so

[88] *Sikṣa-samuccaya,* 325; Winternitz, "Der Mahayana-Buddhismus" *op. cit.,* p. 38.

[89] Martin P. Nilsson, *Geschichte der griechischen Religion* (Munich, 1941), I, 392.

[90] *Mahavagga,* VIII, 26, 4; Winternitz, *Der ältere Buddhismus,* p. 141.

[91] Clement of Alexandria *Stromateis* i. 19, 94; ii, 15, 70; Tertullian *De oratione,* p. 26.

[92] Heiler, "Der ganze Christus," in *Im Ringen um die Kirche* (Munich, 1931), pp. 34 f.; *Mysterium caritatis* (Munich, 1949), pp. 418 ff., 466 f.

[93] Heiler, *Im Ringen,* p. 224; *Mysterium caritatis,* p. 418.

[94] *Sermon on the 18th Sunday after Trinity, 1526* (Erlangen ed.), XVII, 260.

[95] *Gītañjali,* 10; *Gesammelte Werke,* ed. Meyer-Benfey and Helene Meyer-Franck (Munich), I, 138.

great a love, the barriers between religions must fall, and if until now they have not fallen, the only reason is that they have not taken seriously the consequences of their most ultimate and profound principles. "Religion is love" (*religion est l'amour*), the much condemned Ernest Renan has very rightly said.[96] Love is the way of proving that there is a God, for God is visible in love. "No man has ever seen God," says John, "if we love one another, God abides in us and his love is perfected in us" (I John 4:12). The mutual love among men is nothing less than the visible manifestation of God.

7. Love is the most superior way to God. On this way all high religions reach out toward the ultimate goal of divine infinity in which all finiteness finds its fulfilment, even though this goal may be visualized in different images. The Kingdom of God, heaven, paradise, the land of happiness (*sukhavati*), Brahmanirvana, and Parinirvana—these are all but various names for one reality, the "highest blessedness" (*paranam sukham*), as the Buddhists say.[97] Though this blessedness now be imagined as a dissolving of the finite into the infinite (the Upanishads compare it to salt dissolving in water,[98] and Buddha compares it to rivers flowing into the sea),[99] or as the vision of the divine countenance or as a uniting of the soul with the heavenly spouse, it is one and the same reality to which the pious soul keeps looking while in this state of finiteness and which it is already anticipating within this finiteness. The "daily entering into the heavenly realm," of which one Upanishad speaks,[100] corresponds to "our commonwealth in heaven" spoken of by the Apostle Paul (Phil. 3:20). This bliss, however, is as the final existence for the lower spirits in the high religions a total and universal one. That is to say, it excludes the cruel and godless idea of the popular belief in an eternal punishment in hell. The merciful bodhisattva vows not to enter blessedness himself until all living things have found redemption.[101] This

[96] Henriette Psichari, *Renan d'après lui-même* (Paris, 1937), p. 131.

[97] Heiler, *Buddhistische Versenkung*, pp. 40, 84.

[98] *Chandogya-Upanishad*, VI, 9; Deussen, *60 Upanishads des Veda* (Leipzig, 1921), p. 166.

[99] *Aṅguttara-Nikaya*, IV, p. 202; *Udāna*, p. 55; Beckh, *op. cit.*, II, 126.

[100] *Chandogya-Upanishad*, VIII, 3, 3; Deussen, *op. cit.*, p. 191.

[101] *Sukhavati-vyuha-Sutra*, *Sacred Books of the East*, Vol. XLIX; Hans Haas, *Amida Buddha unsere Zuflucht* (Leipzig, 1910); also cf. Söderblom, *Natürliche Theologie und allgemeine Religionsgeschichte* (Leipzig, 1914), pp. 103, 3 ff.

doctrine of Mahayana Buddhism is contiguous with the Maz-
dean doctrine of the universe which is ultimately filled only by
divine beings,[102] and with the Christian doctrine of the restora-
tion of all things (*apokatastasis hapanton*) advocated by Origen
(following early Christian gnosticism)[103] and promulgated by the
great Church Fathers of the East, Gregory of Nazianzus and
Gregory of Nyssa, and professed by many Christian saints in
opposition to popular dogmatics.[104]

Thus there is an ultimate and most profound unity of all high
religions, including ancient Buddhism, which, in spite of its apparent antimetaphysical agnosticism, reveals a mystic religion of
redemption equal to the noblest forms of mysticism of all times
and all religions. This unity exists in spite of all differences in
doctrine and cultus; one need not establish this unity artificially
but, like a diver, simply lift up out of the deep that treasure
which rests upon the ocean floor. Occasionally, however, such a
precious treasure emerges on the surface of the water by itself
and is visible to all. "One of the most astounding facts of the history of religions," Max Müller points out,[105] is the admission of
Buddha to the Roman calendar of saints.[106] One of the most
widespread medieval legends of the saints was that of Barlaam
and Joasaph; that is the legend of Buddha entering into the
Eastern as well as the Roman church via Persia, Arabia, Syria,
and Byzantium.[107] St. Joasaph, whose remembrance is annually
observed in the calendar (*Menaean*) of the Greek Orthodox
church as well as in the *Martyrologium Romanum*, is none other
than the Bodhisattva. This occurrence has symbolic meaning; it
proves the validity of the statement of the renowned traveler-
explorer Marco Polo: "If Buddha had been a Christian, he would

[102] *La Vie future d'après le Mazdéisme* ("Annales du Musée Guimet"
[Paris, 1901]), p. 270.

[103] I Cor. 15:28.

[104] Carl Schneider, *Geistestgeschichte des antiken Christentums*, I, 466.

[105] Will Hayes, *How the Buddha Became a Christian Saint* (Dublin, 1931),
p. 7.

[106] *Selected Essays*, I (1869), 546; cf. *Chips from a German Workshop* (London, 1875), IV, 179–89.

[107] Ernst Kuhn "Barlaam und Joasaph," *Eine bibliographisch-literar-
geschichtliche Studie* (Munich, 1897); cf. H. Gunter, *Buddha in der abend-
ländischen Legende?* (Leipzig, 1922); Hans Haas, *Buddha in der abendlän-
dischen Legende?* (Leipzig, 1923).

have been a great saint of our Lord Jesus Christ, so good and pure was the life that he led."[108] We find such saintly persons in great number in all high religions. And only because the living saints of the various religions are so similar to each other could it happen that the founder of the greatest Eastern religion of redemption was admitted to the throng of canonized Christian saints.

Within the great unity of all high religions, the four prophetic religions of revelation (Judaism, Christianity, Islam, and Zoroastrian Mazdaism) find bonds of even closer unity. Historically they are all closely related to one another. All are monotheistic and ethical religions, and all require daily obligatory prayer of their believers as an act of adoration of Divine Majesty.

The triad of Judaism, Christianity, and Islam is elevated out of this quartet as being one in their faith in God as creator and lawgiver, judge and pardoner, punisher and forgiver. Jewish, Christian, and Muslim piety circles around the poles of sin and grace. The system of parochial worship characteristic of these three religions has one common tradition, inasmuch as the Christian form of worship arose out of the Judaic and the Islamic arose out of both. This is true not only of the form of worship but also of the place of worship. Synagogue, church, and mosque are an architectural unity over against the temples of other religions. They all have a "holy of holies": in the synagogue it is the sacred ark with the Torah scrolls; in the church it is the altar and in the later Roman church the tabernacle; in the mosque it is the prayer niche facing Mecca. There is profound tragedy in the fact that in the history of Christians and Jews, on the one hand, and Christians and Muslims, on the other, there has been so much bitter struggle. And in view of the extremely close religious relationship, this mortal enmity makes no sense whatsoever as it still smolders today between the Jews of Palestine and the Muslim Arabs.

These three religions cherish belief in ecclesiastical institutions and laws, but the legal system in all three has been softened or

[108] *The Book of Sir Marco Polo*, trans. and ed. Sir Henry Yule (London, 1903), II, 318. See also Max Müller, *Chips*, IV, 188: "If he lived the life which is there described, few saints have a better claim to the title than Buddha; and no one either in the Greek or in the Roman Church need be ashamed of having paid to Buddha's memory the honour that was intended for St. Josaphat, the prince, the hermit, and the saint."

entirely overcome by a profound and pure mysticism in which the highest goal is the unity of the soul with the eternal God. The history of the personal piety of these religions is largely a history of mysticism of the speculative-theological kind as well as the mysticism which expresses itself in simple prayers. The Jewish Kabbala and Chassidism, as well as Muslim Sufism, reveal a surprising similarity to Christian mysticism, and this mysticism in turn weaves a bond of unity around the related forms of mysticism which constitute the heart of the great Eastern religions of redemption—Taoism, Brahmanism, Hinduism, and Buddhism.[109]

Still closer than the trinity of these three prophetic religions of redemption is the unity of Christianity and its mother religion of Israel. Jesus is the fulfilment of the preaching of the prophets of Israel. The Christian community owes to Judaism not only the idea of a creation of the world from nothing, the prophetic faith in God's revelation in history, the intensity of a knowledge of sin, the trust in God's forgiving grace, the expectation of the Kingdom of God, and prayer as the "outpouring of the heart," but also its most sacred sacrament. The parting meal of Jesus in Jerusalem, from which emerged the mystery meal of the New Covenant, was a Jewish meal. Its designation as "eucharist" is only the Greek rendition of the Jewish term *berākhā*, that is, blessing and thanksgiving over bread and wine. When in a Jewish service of worship on the Sabbath eve I see the elevated kiddusch-cup and hear the words, "Blessed art Thou who givest us the fruit of the vine," then I always see at the same time the chalice which is elevated by the Christian priest in the eucharistic liturgy. Though the navel cord may have been torn at the birth of Christianity, the church of the New Covenant is yet bound to the people of God of the Old Covenant in the same indissoluble unity as a child with its mother. For that reason the Christian church has never ceased to use the Jewish psalter as its foremost book of prayer. Indeed, the most sacred prayer of Christendom, the Lord's Prayer, is but a summary and concentration of the prayers used by the Jews of the time of Jesus.

With respect to this great unity of the high religions, one can only repeat the prayer of Cardinal Nicolas of Cusa: "It is Thou,

---

[109] Cf. Heiler, *Die Bedeutung der Mystik für die Weltreligionen* (Munich, 1919).

O God, who is being sought in the various religions in various ways, and named with various names, for Thou remainest as Thou art, to all incomprehensible and inexpressible. Be gracious and show Thy countenance. . . . When Thou wilt graciously perform it, then the sword, jealous hatred, and all evil will cease and all will come to know that there is but *one* religion in the variety of religious customs [*una religio in rituum varietate*]."[110]

One of the most important tasks of the science of religion is to bring to light this unity of all religions. It thereby pursues only one purpose, that of pure knowledge of the truth. But unintentionally there sprouts forth from the root of scientific inquiry into truth a tree not only with wondrous blossoms but also with glorious fruit. When Helmholz discovered the eye-mirror a century ago, he was pursuing no practical medical purpose but only a theoretical research purpose. But through his research zeal he brought help to millions who suffer with eye disease. The same is true of the scientific study of religion. Its inquiry into truth bears important consequences for the practical relationship of one religion to another. Whoever recognizes their unity must take it seriously by tolerance in word and deed. Thus scientific insight into this unity calls for a practical realization in friendly exchange and in common ethical and social endeavor which the British call "fellowship" and "co-operation."

This unity and this fellowship are as little a syncretistic mixing of religion as is a conversion from one system of religion to another. Schleiermacher's *Reden* contains the sincere warning:

If you want to compare religion with religion as the eternally progressing work of the world spirit, you must give up the vain and futile wish that there ought to be only one; your antipathy against the variety of religions must be laid aside, and with as much impartiality as possible you must join all those which have developed from the eternally abundant bosom of the Universe through the changing forms and progressive traditions of man.[111]

Rabindranath Tagore agrees with this warning against antipathy toward the diversity of religions and the will of one religion to dominate. He states:

The attempt to make their own religion the ruling one everywhere and for all time is natural to men who incline toward a sectarianism. Therefore they do not want to hear that God is magnanimous in the

---

[110] *De pace seu concordantia fidei, loc. cit.*
[111] *Reden*, Rede 5, 241, p. 123.

dispensing of His love, or that His dealings with men are not limited to one blind alley which comes to a sudden halt at one point in history. If ever such a catastrophe should break in upon mankind that one religion should swamp everything, then God would have to provide a second Noah's ark to save his creatures from spiritual destruction.[112]

Joy in the individuality of another religion is the ultimate joy in God Himself. Schleiermacher asked whether Christianity was destined to be the only religion of mankind. Evidently he held that Christianity was against this despotism. It is not a main tenet of Christianity to seek uniformity in religion by destroying other religious systems. Rather it honors all forms of religious expression because all have necessary ingredients for what Schleiermacher considers "the religion of all religions." However, Schleiermacher judged this too optimistically. Not many Christian theologians have followed him in this, but among them are to be found such men of renown as Nathan Söderblom and Rudolf Otto. Most Christian theologians fear nothing so much as "relativism." I have a way of answering such theologians that the greatest of all relativists is God himself, the Absolute, for he is fulness in itself and his fulness is revealed in the immeasurable diversity of nature and the spiritual life.

Toynbee, in the book mentioned above, recalls the wonderful statement that the defender of dying pagan religion, Quintus Aurelius Symmachus, used against the church father, Ambrosius, "The heart of so great a mystery can never be reached by following only one way."[113] To this Toynbee adds the comment:

We can take the statement of Symmachus to our hearts without being disloyal to Christianity, but we cannot harden our hearts against Symmachus without hardening them against Christ; for what Symmachus preached is Christian love of which the Apostle says that it will never cease. Though there be prophecies, they shall pass away, and though there be tongues they will cease, though there be knowledge, it will pass away.[114]

The deeper our reverence for God, the deeper also must our reverence for other religions be. More than two thousand years ago, King Asoka, Buddha's zealous disciple, made it clear to his people that whoever honors another religion honors his own, and

[112] "Lebensweisheit," in *Gesammelte Werke*, VIII, 282.

[113] *Relatio Symmachi*, ed. Seeck, 6, 1, p. 282; under the works of Ambrose, in Migne, *Patrologia Latina*, XVI, 966 ff.

[114] *An Historian's Approach to Religion*, p. 297.

whoever disgraces another disgraces his own. His admonition still holds good for our day. He who has penetrated the mystery of religion will cease wanting simply to convert the believers among the other high religions; moreover, his desire is twofold, to give and to receive, to represent the purest form of Christianity to others and in turn to learn about the most intimate character of the belief of others. He does not want to conquer those religions, but unite with them at a higher level. He would not "destroy" them but "fulfil" them (Matt. 5:17); he does not want their death, but (as Rudolf Otto said) he wants no religion to die before its ultimate and most profound meaning has been told.[115] The meaning of true mission is not propaganda or conversion or domination of others but brotherly exchange and brotherly competition.[116] In this sense we must not only wish that Christian mission continue among the religions of the East (Max Müller said that for every missionary he would rather send out ten more), but also that the religions of the East send missionaries to us,[117] as Leibniz had already desired in the introduction to his *Novissima Sinica*.[118] Such a mission does not lead to syncretism and eclecticism but to "such growth in the essentials" as Asoka had demanded from the different religions, and that means nothing other than growth in love toward God and man.

On this basis there naturally follows a co-operation of religions in "life and work," to extend this expression which Söderblom used of the Christian ecumenical communion to the ecumenical union of all religions.[119] In the last decades various

[115] *Vishnu-Narayana*, p. 224.

[116] H. Frick, *Die evangelische Mission, Ursprung, Geschichte, Ziel* (Bonn, 1922), pp. 449 ff.; and particularly the famous address on missions by Max Müller, "Westminster Lecture on Missions," 3, 12 (1872), in *Chips from a German Workshop* (London, 1875), IV, 251–80. Cf. Söderblom, *Missionens Motiv och kulturvärde in ur religionens historia* (Stockholm, 1915), p. 194: "Mission means that the encounter between the great human cultural types, that is the great powers of human ideas, becomes as deep and central and many-sided as possible." Heiler, "Die Mission des Christentums in Indien," in *Rudolf Otto Festgruss*, 5 (Gotha, 1931).

[117] *Chips from a German Workshop*, IV, 354.

[118] *Novissima Sinica, historiam nostri temporis illustratura in quibus de christianismo publica nunc primum autoritate propagato missa in Europam relatio exhibetur, deque favore scientiarum Europaearum*, etc. (2d ed., 1699). The first edition appeared anonymously in 1697.

[119] Cf. Heiler, "Mut zur Liebe," in *Die Zusammenarbeit der Religionen im Dienste der ganzen Menschheit* (Lecture in the "Week of Brotherhood"), *Eine heilige Kirche* (1953–54), pp. 18–33.

organizations have grown up on this basis, such as the Universal Religious Alliance, International Religious Peace Conference, World Parliament of Religions, World Congress for Free Christianity and Religious Progress, Union of All Religions, World Congress of Faiths, and Fraternity of Religious Mankind, founded by Rudolf Otto.[120] In 1956 this latter organization joined the World Congress of Faiths founded by Sir Francis Younghusband as the German branch. The World Harmony founded by Hossein Kazemzadeh Iranschähr[121] serves a similar purpose. None of these movements aims at an unorganic syncretism of religions. No, each religion shall continue to unfold its individuality. But through friendship and common co-operation among the religions we develop mankind more and more. All high religions are distinguished from the lower nationalistic religions of mankind.[122] They have realized only imperfectly, however, the concept of humanity toward which they strive because they have detached themselves from other religions striving for the same goal and because they have looked upon one another as competitors or even as enemies instead of brethren and children of the same family of God.

If the religions thus learn to understand one another and co-operate, they will contribute more to the realization of humanity and thereby to world peace than all the noteworthy efforts of politics. A torn humanity which has passed through so many catastrophes, which has ruined itself through so many wars, which is still bleeding from so many wounds, can be saved by one thing only, which is rooted in and proceeds from divine love as it lives in the high religions, primarily in their saints and martyrs. Co-operation in the conquest of racial, national, economic, and social problems will by itself lead to the securing and maintaining of world peace. Responsibility before the eternal God and selfless love for one's brother, these alone warrant the greatest security.

---

[120] R. Otto, "Religiöser Menschheitsbund neben politischem Völkerbund," *Christliche Welt*, No. 9 (1920); "Religiöser Menschheitsbund," *Religion in Geschichte und Gegenwart* (1929), III, 1222.

[121] *Weltharmonie: Wegweiser zur Lebensharmonie und zum Weltfrieden, Gründer und Redaktor*, ed. K. H. Iranschähr (Winterthur: W. Baltensberger, 1957), ninth Annual.

[122] Cf. Heiler, "Die Bedeutung der Religionen für die Entwicklung des Menschheits—und Friedensgedankens," *Oekumenische Einheit*, II, No. 1, 1–29.

Satyāgraha (the apprehension of truth), *ahimsā* (the inviolability of all life), *parātmā-samata* (the identity of all alien spirits), *parātmā-nirvana* (the self-transformation into an alien soul), *mahāmaitrī* (great, all-encompassing love), and *mahā-karunā* (great compassion) are age-old religious ideals which Indian saints realized centuries before Christ and which Gandhi put into practice anew in our century.[123] Gandhi is likewise an example for the unity of religions. He drew not only from the treasure store of his Indian forefathers, from the Upanishads and the Bhagavad-gita, but also from the Koran and the New Testament, mainly from the Sermon on the Mount. He believed in the mysterious unity of divine revelation in all high religions. Upon hearing the statement of a Christian missionary, the Rev. Anstein of Basel, "I take you also to be a disciple of Jesus," he answered, "That I am indeed, but in a sense other than you believe; for I regard myself as a disciple of Buddha, Muhammad, and Krishna as well. They all want one and the same thing, truth and love."[124] In his Ashram, a co-operation has been realized among the circle of his friends even in common worship among members of different religions. As earlier in the worship services of the *Brāhmosamāj*, which emerged from Hinduism, and of the Bahāi and Sūfī groups, which emerged from Persian Islam, portions from the various bibles of mankind were read in these services of worship. The same occurred also in the worship services of the sessions of the World Congress of Faiths. First the believers of the various religions listened to the Word of God in the various sacred scriptures of mankind and then in holy silence hearkened to the inner Word of God. In the worship of the Sūfī these sacred scriptures lie upon the altar on which stand seven candlesticks. At the beginning of the service the candles are lit one after the other, each a symbol of one of the high religions except the seventh, which is the symbol of those seekers after God who belong to no religion. That there can also be a liturgical fellowship of believers from different religions was shown at the conclusion of the World Congress for Free Christianity and Religious Progress in

[123] Cf. Heiler, *Christlicher Glaube und indisches Geistesleben* (Munich, 1926), pp. 37–51; W. E. Mühlmann, *Mahatma Gandhi, der Mann, sein Werk und seine Wirkung* (Tübingen, 1950).

[124] Hans Anstein with Heiler, *Die Wahrheit Sundar Singhs, Neue Dokumente zum Sadhustreit* (Munich, 1927), p. 201.

Berlin (1910),[125] when Père Hyacinthe Loyson, a former Carmelite monk, led in the Lord's Prayer, and Jews, Muslims, Hindus, Sikhs, and Buddhists joined him, some with and some without words.

A new era will dawn upon mankind when the religions will rise to true tolerance and co-operation in behalf of mankind. To assist in preparing the way for this era is one of the finest hopes of the scientific study of religion. It was this hope that possessed one of its greatest pioneers, Friedrich Max Müller. Therefore, this essay will be concluded with the same words of the last hymn of the Ṛgveda to Agni (X, 191) with which Max Müller closed his inaugural address as president of the Arian section of the International Oriental Congress in London in 1874:

> United come, united speak, let your spirits agree . . . !
> Let your efforts united be; unite your hearts!
> Let your spirit united be, by which you are firmly bound. . . .
> Peace, peace, peace.[126]

In the original language and in the solemn manner of recitation of ancient India this verse resounds yet more fully:

> Saṃ gacchadhvaṃ sam vadadhvam sam vah manāṃsi jānatām . . .
> Samānī vaḥ ākūtiḥ samānā hṛdayāni vaḥ,
> Samānam astu vaḥ manah, yathā vaḥ susaha asati.
> Shānti, Shānti, Shānti.

[125] *World Congress for Free Christianity and Religious Progress, Protocol of Discussions* (Berlin, 1910).

[126] *Chips from a German Workshop*, IV, 371.

Biographical Notes

ERNST BENZ, professor of church history and historical theology, and also Director of Ecumenical Studies at the University of Marburg in Germany, was born in 1907 and educated at the universities of Tübingen, Berlin, and Rome. He was on the faculty of the University of Halle-Wittenberg from 1932 to 1935, when he assumed his present position. He is a regular participant in the Eranos Lectures. His writings cover a broad range of subjects, including such titles as *Ecclesia Spiritualis, Emanuel Swedenborg,* and *Die Abendländische Sendung der östlich-orthodoxen Kirche.* Professor Benz is coeditor of the *Zeitschrift für Religions- und Geistesgeschichte.*

JEAN DANIÉLOU, S.J., is professor of the history of Christian origins at the Catholic Institute of Paris. He is also director of the collection, *Sources Chrétiennes.* He is a frequent lecturer at the Eranos meetings and in 1958 he gave the Sarun Lectures at Oxford University. Among his recent publications are *Dieu et nous, Les Saints païens de l'Ancien Testament, La Théologie du Judéo-christianisme, Les manuscrits de la Mer Morte et les origines chrétiennes,* and an English translation of *Origen.* In preparation at the time this volume was published is a work on the interrelationship of Christianity and Hellenism in the apologists and Clement of Alexandria. Father Daniélou is also interested in problems of church union and international community.

MIRCEA ELIADE, born in Romania in 1907, is chairman of the history of religions field at the Federated Theological Faculty of the University of Chicago. He has also taught at the University of Bucharest and at the École des Hautes Études (Sorbonne) in Paris. He is a regular participant in the annual Eranos Lectures at Ascona, Switzerland. In addition to several scholarly works and novels not yet translated into English, his works include *The Myth of the Eternal Return (Cosmos and History), The Sacred and the Profane, Patterns in Comparative Religion, Birth and Rebirth* (Haskell Lectures, 1956), and *Yoga— Immortality and Freedom.*

FRIEDRICH HEILER was born in Munich in 1892. He holds a Ph.D. from the University of Munich, Th.D. (honorary) from Kiel University, and D.D. from the University of Glasgow. He has been professor of the history of religions at the University of Marburg since 1920 and

161

is also president of the German branch of the International Association for the History of Religions. He has also held the titles of president of the High Church (now Evangelical-Ecumenical) Union of Germany, director of the Religionskundliche Sammlung of the University of Marburg, and vice-president of the German branch of the World Congress of Faiths. In 1955 he delivered the Haskell Lectures at the University of Chicago. He is the editor of the journals *Eine heilige Kirche* and *Die Hochkirche*. Dr. Heiler is the author of *Prayer* (*Das Gebet*), *Buddhistische Versenkung, Die Mystik der Upanishaden, Sadhu Sundar Singh* (English edition, 1926), *Der Katholizismus, Urkirche und Ostkirche, Altkirchliche Autonomie und päpstlicher Zentralismus, Die Religionen der Menschheit in Vergangenheit und Gegenwart.*

JOSEPH M. KITAGAWA, born in Osaka, Japan, in 1915, has been teaching in the history of religions field at the University of Chicago since 1951. He also serves as adviser in this field for the *Encyclopaedia Britannica*. During the 1958–59 academic year he was engaged in extensive research in Buddhism and other Eastern religions in the countries of the Far East and southeast Asia. In the summer of 1958 he lectured in the Department of Buddhist Studies at Koyasan University in Japan and took an active part in the Ninth Congress of the International Association for the History of Religions at Tokyo. He edited the posthumous work by Joachim Wach, *The Comparative Study of Religions,* and *Modernity and World Religions* (the 1957 Paul Carus Memorial Symposium).

LOUIS MASSIGNON is a French historian and orientalist who for many years held the chair of Islamic sociology at the Collège de France and taught at the École des Hautes Études in Paris. He is General Secretary for the Comité France-Islam, a member of the Russian Academy of Sciences and of the Royal Academies of Copenhagen, Teheran, Stockholm, Amsterdam, Brussels, Kabul, and Cairo, the Academy of Damascus, the Royal Asiatic Society of London, the Deutsche Morgenländische Gesellschaft, and the American Oriental Society and Asian Society. He was Haskell lecturer at the University of Chicago in 1952. Professor Massignon is the editor of the *Revue des Études Islamiques* and the *Annuaire du Monde Musulman*. His books include *La passion d'al Hallâj, Martyr mystique d'Islam, Expérience mystique et stylisation littéraire, Le Diwan d'al Hallâj, Les Sept Dormants d'Éphèse, Un vœu et un destin: Marie Antoinette,* and *La mubâhala de Médine et l'hyperdulie de Fâtima.*

RAFFAELE PETTAZZONI, born in 1883, has been professor of the history of religions at the University of Rome since 1924. In 1951 he became president of the International Association for the History of Religions and is also the editor of its journal, *Numen*. He is the author of a large number of books and articles on comparative religion, including *The All-Knowing God* (*L'onniscienza di Dio*), *La confessione dei peccati,*

Essays in the History of Religions, La religione nella Grecia antica, La religione di Zarathustra, I misteri, and *Miti e Leggende.* Professor Pettazzoni is a member of several European learned societies and holds honorary degrees from the universities of Brussels and Strasbourg.

Wilfred Cantwell Smith is W. M. Birks Professor of Comparative Religion at McGill University, Montreal, Canada, and has also been Director of the Institute of Islamic Studies at that University since its establishment in 1952. He was born in Toronto in 1916. He traveled and lived in South America, Europe, and the Near East before entering the University of Toronto, where he studied oriental languages and history. He studied theology at Westminster College, Cambridge, and holds a doctorate in Oriental Studies from Princeton University. He taught Islamic and Indian history at Forman Christian College, Lahore. A scholar of Islam, Professor Smith has published numerous articles and two books: *Modern Islam in India* and *Islam in Modern History.*

163

Acknowledgments

The publication of this collection of essays would not have been possible had it not been for the encouragement of many friends of the late Joachim Wach, especially Dean Jerald C. Brauer and members of the Federated Theological Faculty of the University of Chicago. The editors wish to express their gratitude to the many friends and colleagues who have helped to prepare this work. Dr. Wilhelm Wuellner and the Reverend Dean Lueking translated the German articles by Professors Benz and Heiler. The French articles by Professors Eliade, Daniélou, and Massignon were translated by a committee consisting of Dr. John Hirschfield, Mr. Cornelis Bolle, and Mrs. Kathryn Atwater. Mr. Lucio Chiaraviglio made the translation from Italian of Professor Pettazzoni's essay.

We are very grateful to Mrs. Kathryn Atwater, who as editorial assistant handled all the correspondence, prepared the manuscript for publication, and read the proofs.

The gracious and helpful co-operation of the secretarial staff of the University of Chicago Divinity School is also gratefully acknowledged. Mrs. Minerva Bell, Mrs. Rehova Arthur, and Miss Gloria Valentine, among others, typed and proofread many of the articles.